The Ancient Art of Faery Magick

D. J. Conway

CROSSING PRESS
Berkeley

All rights reserved. Published in the United States by Crossing Press, an imprint of
the Crown Publishing Group, a division of Random House, Inc., New York.
www.crownpublishing.com
www.tenspeed.com

Crossing Press and the Crossing Press colophon are registered trademarks of
Random House, Inc.

Library of Congress Cataloging-in-Publication Data

Conway, D. J. (Deanna J.)
  The ancient art of faery magick / D.J. Conway.
    p. cm.
  Includes bibliographical references and index.
  1. Fairies. I. Title.
  BF1552.C66 2005
  398'.45—dc22

ISBN 13: 978-1-58091-157-3

Cover design by Rebecca S. Neimark, Twenty-Six Letters
Text design by Chloe Rawlins

146119709

The
Ancient Art
of
Faery Magick

This book is dedicated to my beloved Charles, a man of great integrity, dignity, love, and absolute belief in the Fay and the Small Folk. His sense of joy and humor matched theirs, and taught me to love him, life, and the faeries more than I thought possible.

It is also dedicated to Jeanne and Steve, who helped me put my life together again after my loss. Their little family is a great blessing in my life. As is Sara Camilli, agent extraordinaire and beloved friend, who encouraged me constantly to keep writing and make a new life for myself.

Also to Sergeant Alan Ubbens, who is putting his life on the line for all of us.

FAERIES

Deep in the shadowy forest
By the stream in the fern-covered glen,
The strong Faery Folk live by the oak,
Away from the haunts of men.

They are tall and robust and fearless.
Their long locks all shades of the trees,
From buttercup bright to the blackness of night.
Their bright eyes like changeable leaves.

Some still fall in love with a human
And pledge them their love for all time.
Great vistas shown to their lover alone.
Their voices are joyful, sublime.

They deal with intruders most harshly.
Their knowledge and kingdom protect.
Unbelievers, beware! They will fill you with fear.
A deep panic they're known to project.

A race rich in wisdom and legend,
Faeries once shared their knowledge with all,
But withdrew to the glens, the mountains, and fens,
Where they built up invisible walls.

For humankind proved to be treacherous,
Unworthy of friendship and lore.
The Faery Folk wait at their Otherworld gate
For those worthy to come to their door.

Belief is the key to admittance
To their knowledge, both wondrous and old.
The reluctant and shy don't believe and won't try.
Faery power must be used by the bold.

Faery power reaches deep into earth soil,
Upward to planets and each star.
It rolls with the seas and harnesses the breeze.
Those who learn it can all travel far.

Acceptance by Faery Folk changes you.
You learn to be one with the All,
For their power is great. Yield to your fate.
Have no regrets when you answer their call.

—D. J. Conway

Contents

Introduction: My Life with Magick and Faeries   xi

What is a Faery?   1

How to Find Faeries and Befriend Them   9

Opening the Door to the Faery World   37

The Fay   49

The Small Folk   73

Faeries of Earth   93

Faeries of Air   99

Faeries of Water   101

Faeries of Fire   105

Faeries of Plants and Forests   109

Faeries of the Deserts   113

House Faeries   117

Faery Kith and Kin   127

The Secret Faery Oracle   155

Faery Gardens   159

Faery Houses and Sacred Places   167

Stories for Adults and Children   173

Recommended Reading   209

Index   215

My Life with Magick and Faeries

In my sixty-five-plus years in this life, I can remember only a very few times when I was not aware of the power of magick, faeries, elves, dragons, and many other extraordinary creatures that most other people did not see. I was also aware that the power of magick, in its many different forms, was connected with these beings and the Otherworld.

As a child, I was instinctively aware that these things were real, for I learned to use the magick to see into the past and the future—and, on occasion, I made events happen that should have been beyond my ability to influence. Since few others in my family acknowledged their talents in this area, I learned quickly that I would be punished if I talked about any of this. *Silence* was the key word for generations. If you didn't talk about such strange happenings, then society would not look at you as if you were crazy or ignorant and superstitious. My beloved paternal grandmother was the only one who talked to me about sensing future events, telepathy, healing, and of course the Small Folk. Perhaps that was because I was so full of questions and she was the only one who never punished me for asking them.

As a child, I was very wary of the Fay, for I had been told they sometimes stole away children who had the second sight. I watched them from afar, listening to their talks among themselves, and envious of their weapons and wonderful outfits. Now I realize that the Fay knew all the time that I was eavesdropping, and were using this method to instruct me in small magicks that a child could use without harming others.

However, it was the Small Folk and their sensational nature magick that drew me to the forests and meadows and creeks again and again. In fact, as often as I could slip away alone, I wandered these silent, peaceful areas, watching and learning from the Faery Folk. I suppose that or, because they were smaller than I was, I had no fear of them. I shared the first wild strawberries with them by the shaded creek. I marveled at the brilliant colors of sunset over the pond where the wild ducks often sought shelter.

It did not take me long to learn that at certain hours and times of the year it was easier to see and mingle with the Faery Folk. I watched for them at dawn, noon, dusk, and midnight. Although in those days I was not Wiccan/Pagan, I discovered that faeries made special appearances on eight particular days of the year. Later, I learned what these days were called. Faeries appear in greater numbers at Imbolc (February 1), the spring equinox in March, Beltane (May 1), the summer solstice in June, Lunasa (August 1), the autumn equinox in September, Samhain (October 31), and the winter solstice in December.

I found that many people new to the Craft, especially children, had difficulty remembering what each of the special days meant. I finally settled on writing a series of eight short stories, one for each of the days, that explained through actions of characters what that day and part of the season meant. Parents and others have asked me for years to put all the stories into a book. I am very happy to say that all eight stories are included at the end of this book.

As I grew older, between schoolwork and farmwork my alone time was cut to almost nothing. Mundane worldly things began to fill my days, while the Small Folk, the Fay, and their magickal teachings slid into the background. When I began my own family, I was caught in the generations-old dilemma of talking to my children about the psychic, the Scots/Irish second sight, while my husband believed in nothing. I chose to secretly answer my children's questions and to help them understand as much as I could about these happenings. By doing this, I cracked open the door to my own locked-away psychic senses. These crept out, one by one, until the door was wide open again.

I had a psychic-spiritual thirst that was nearly overwhelming. I began to study Eastern religions, New Age teachings (which were hard to come by at that time), the tarot, runes, all methods of nonorthodox healing, meditation, Wicca, and of course magick. The Faery Folk and elves swarmed back into my chaotic life, teaching me, warning me, and at last leading me to the Lady, the Goddess, the female half of the pair of deities that made the universe and everything in it. I jumped into ancient history and mythology, tracing each clue to the Goddess and the God as far back as I could, which I finally concluded started in the Stone Age. I did my own self-initiation into Wicca, or the Old Path as I called it, long before it was popular in the United States to do so.

I studied and walked this magickal path alone until 1975, when suddenly I realized that there were others out there who believed the same. I no longer had to remain silent. In fact, I discovered a number of groups, whose beliefs were not all exactly the same, but who had enough of the basics for me to be comfortable being with them. It did not take long to notice the infighting for control and quarrels over who was right and who was wrong in these groups. So I went back to my solitary Old Path and began to write books that I hoped would help others—books to help people learn magick and the truth about the Faery Folk and other beings, books that would help them to help themselves. People needed to know that they could chose a spiritual path just right for them without requiring the "bless-ing" of a group to be authentic.

Every day I learn something new from the Faery Folk. This learning isn't all spectacular material but usually mundane, practical things that make life a little easier and happier.

A colorful piece of paper doesn't make you anything other than what you are inside.

The Small Folk were always with me, celebrating the eight holy days, and more often teasing and playing tricks. Only one time did they appear as golden lights in a photograph. I had my back to the camera, and all around the top edge of the walls of the room was a precisely spaced string of yellow lights. I was skeptical at first, looking for all mundane types of explanations such as things that would reflect light, but there was no explanation. Like Sherlock Holmes, when I exhausted all possible explanations, I had to accept the impossible as true.

Now it is nothing for me to see the Small Folk zip past the corner of my eye, or catch a glimpse of a tall dark shadow of a Fay watching, perhaps overseeing, what I am doing. They tease the cats, who chase them as they would butterflies, then look surprised when the Small Ones suddenly disappear. My house and life would be empty without them.

By attracting and welcoming the Good Small Folk, I rarely find any of the troublemakers residing in my house—and none of those obnoxious creatures stay very long.

I have lived so long with magick and the Faery Folk that acknowledging them or working unobtrusively with magick has become a common practice for me. I rarely get out the "big guns," as I call the wide variety of ritual tools I have. Those are saved for the very tough and important magicks. I work more with silent chants, visualization, candle burning, burnt papers, or the undetected transfer of energy through a touch, a hug, or a kiss. The Faery Folk know that all of these methods work quite well, and they are willing to help at any time. And they continue to be noisy observers of each book I write, as they were with this one, offering opinions, suggestions, and warnings.

I cannot imagine a life without magick or members of the Faery Folk. It would be a colorless, uninteresting world to me. So long live the faeries! After all, they have been here longer than humans.

chapter 1

What Is a Faery?

Do you remember how, as a child, you believed in faeries and other invisible fantastical folk? And how, as you got older, you were talked out of their reality? Well, faeries actually do exist—partly in the Otherworld, or astral realm, and partly in this physical world. They are not imaginary creatures but another type of physical/ethereal being. Because we have been taught that faeries are only fantasy, as adults we refuse to see them or acknowledge their existence.

Faery bodies are formed of the same basic materials as are humans, and most of them look very much like us. They can become visible or invisible by changing the vibrational rate of their bodies. Although they are a different species of being, with abilities different from those of humans, they are similar to us in many ways. Old stories tell of how, on occasion, the human-size faeries whom I call the Fay would intermarry with humans and produce children.

Faeries are not elementals or sprites, although too many people seem to think they are. Like tigers and domestic cats, these different beings are related but certainly are

Since faeries are connected to the earth, they chose to stay connected with its inhabitants but moved their main living quarters into another realm of existence called the Faery Realm or Faery Land.

not the same creatures. Elementals, for example, can work only within the element to which they are attached: Fire, Earth, Air, or Water, whereas faeries can work within and with all elements. Elementals do not have a society and laws, as faeries do. In certain times, humans unable to differentiate between the species have mistakenly given a single name to elementals and faeries. One must therefore read the old tales carefully and learn to distinguish between the species by their actions and habits.

Long ago, faeries lived in closer proximity with humans. However, humans were—and still are—prone to hunt or fear and persecute anyone or anything different from themselves. Faeries were quick to learn that most humans could not be trusted.

By controlling the vibrational rate of their forms, they could remain invisible and still go about their earthly duties. Able to control whether or not they are seen, faeries easily step from their present Otherworld home to the human plane of existence. In other words, they have the ability to move back and forth between worlds in the form of highly tuned energy that usually makes them invisible to us. Those humans aware of faery existence often see their quick movements as a flash of light or movement out of the corner of an eye.

Faeries in one form or another were known to all ancient cultures around the world. They have been on Earth longer than humans. Legends, folklore, and personal historical accounts are full of faery encounters, as well as descriptions of their Otherworld culture and magickal powers. Christianized tales say they are a type of fallen angel, although Christians never called them outright demons until the modern era. However, faeries are neither angels nor humans, but a species unto themselves.

The names by which they were known vary from culture to culture. In Old French, they were called *faer-ees*; in Greece and Rome, they were known as the fates, faes, or fays. The Arabic countries knew them as djinns (genies) and afrits. The Scottish divided them into two groups, the *Seelie Court* and *Unseelie Court*, and called their members the *sith* ("shee"); the Irish name for faeries is nearly the same, *sidhe* (also "shee"). Rather than court faery wrath by unknowingly disrespecting them, most European humans called them the Gentry, the Gentle Folk, the Good Folk, the Fair Folk, or the Ancient Ones.

One specific group of faeries is human-size or larger; others are the tiny ones widely portrayed during the Victorian era. Children often see the tiny winged faeries; my children used to call them "flutterbees." In this book I call them the *Small Folk* and the human-size faeries, the *Fay*, to differentiate them from the smaller, more primitive faeries. The actual term *faery*, however, refers to the entire species of beings. Their world is called Faery Land.

Some faeries were considered "good" or friendly to humans, whereas others were considered unfriendly. There are positive and negative creatures in all species, and faeries are no exception. Some of them became unfriendly to humans because of past experiences with our unreliable species. Some were unfriendly from the beginning, and these are the ones you particularly don't want to offend—and definitely do not want to deliberately contact.

I will use the Scottish terms *Seelie* and *Unseelie Courts* to help the reader understand the difference between the two types of Fay. The Seelie Court, or Blessed Court, is composed of more human-friendly Fay; the Unseelie Court, or Unblessed, are more human-unfriendly. The two courts seldom intermingle, except on rare occasions and for specific reasons. The Unseelie Court, while unfriendly, is not evil; that was propaganda put out by an orthodox religious establishment that saw everything different as a threat to its rule.

Christianity, Islam, and certain aspects of Judaism believe that faeries are lesser, fallen angels who followed Satan and were thrown out of heaven during the great battle. Since faery laws and ideas are quite different from those of humans, humans had long had a healthy respect for faeries and their powers. The new religions played on this respect and turned it to fear—transforming the once awe-inspiring image of faeries into one of demons and evil spirits. These cultures had had direct contact with faeries for generations and knew positively that they existed. Traditions say that faeries, rather than being embittered by their new negative image, rejoiced in the wonder of the earth and the humans who lived there. Outwardly, under the new religious order human cultures appeared to accept the new explanation, but secretly they continued to practice the old ways of interacting with and appeasing the Faery Folk.

All faeries were once treated with respect because they live by different rules, have magickal powers, and hold the key to valuable ancient knowledge. In the past, faeries have given certain humans important information about healing, music, and the other arts and sciences. There are records of powerful human doctors and musicians who were taught their special knowledge by faeries; for example, the tune of "Londonderry Air" was given to an Irish harpist by the faeries, as was the Scottish MacCrimmons' superb bagpipe ability.

The Goddess and the God appointed the Fay, elves, and Small Folk to be custodians of nature, overseeing the worldly work of all the subspecies of their kind, as well as the earth itself. Some of the faery kith and kin appear to have no certain work to do. Many of the faeries and subspecies have formed their own special places among humans, some helpful, some otherwise. (For much more about faery kith and kin, see chapter 13.)

The elusive brownie of the Celts, the hearth-loving domovoi of eastern Europe, the *peris* of Persia, and the tiny *menehunes* of Hawaii are examples of friendly spirits. Irish leprechauns, pixies, and the djinn of Arabia are tricksters around whom it is wise to be cautious. Goblins and gremlins, among others, should be treated with extreme caution and never invited onto your property or into your home.

Properly approached and befriended, today faeries are still open to helping humans. It is important to know how faeries live, their rules of behavior when interacting with humans, how to distinguish between the "friendly" and "unfriendly," how to approach them and entice them into your life, and how to get them to teach you their specialized form of magick to better your life. Chants and spells, when worked with faeries, can improve every facet of your life, from love and health to peace and prosperity.

Faeries age, although much more slowly than humans do. The older faeries have lived for centuries. They can become ill, have difficult childbirths, become injured, or even die. They are very fond of jewelry and fine clothes, music, dancing, riding horses, weapons, exquisite banquets, hounds, and, depending on the clan, even cats. They can speak any human language in the world, even the extinct ones. They can also communicate with every species of creation, whether astral or physical, animate or inanimate, and they are adept at telepathy, teleportation, and reading minds. Their knowledge of magick is nearly equal to that of dragons but is more nature oriented and answers to physical needs.

> *Faeries are intelligent astral beings who can change shape at will, appear and disappear in the blink of an eye, and operate at frequencies beyond our vision and hearing.*

Faeries do not like certain actions and items, and may even be repelled by them. Iron is poisonous to the Faery Folk, so the introduction of iron and its wide use drove most faeries away from human civilization and into the vast woodland of nature. The practice of mounting a horseshoe over a house or stable door stems from the faery dislike of iron—and their love of horses. All faeries, but especially the Small Folk, have a deep affection for and affinity with all horses of any color or size, though they prefer white ones. Faeries frequently "borrow" horses at night to use on their Faery Rides and hunts—so humans sometimes hammered iron horseshoes or patterns of nails onto the stable doors to keep them out. Faeries also have their own faery horses, upon which they lavish much care and attention. Some people have been fortunate enough to be invited to ride on faery horses for a visit to Faery Land.

At each solstice and equinox, plus the four holy days, most faeries travel ancient routes from one living place to another. These processions are called the Faery Rides, Rades (in Scotland), or Cavalcades. These particular routes may have been established many thousands of years ago when faeries first shared the earth with humans. Humans who have any knowledge about faery behavior and customs avoid these routes at the solstices, equinoxes, and four holy days, for it was once not unknown for humans to be taken by the faeries during their rides. Only a very few humans returned, and they were never quite the same again.

Faery Land operates in an entirely different time from that of the physical world—or you could say they do not operate within *any* conception of time, as we know it. Frequently, humans who were temporarily taken into the faery world would discover upon their return that they had been gone for years instead of days. Most of these people spent the rest of their lives longing to return to Faery Land, probably because of the mundane physical existence they had come back to. Any human who spent time in Faery Land was forever changed. Some were granted strong gifts of prophecy or healing. One family in Wales was granted the gift of healing through the sons of a Fay female and a human male; this spectacular gift endured in the family until the 1800s. Usually, however, the faery gift did not extend beyond a single person.

Now is the time for this forgotten area of cultural history to once more be studied and used as it should be. Faery magick is strong, full of love and wonder, and may be just what you need in your hectic life. Faery magick calms the spirit, reconnects you with nature, and opens your heart and mind to the great Otherworld and the supreme power behind all creation. When you open this connection, positive opportunities flow into your life, improving all levels of your existence.

It is also time to acknowledge the existence of the larger human-size faeries, or the Fay, who seem to have been forgotten in favor of the smaller, less powerful faeries. True, interacting with the larger faeries can be dangerous, but no more so than interacting with any other culture on Earth. The main rule to remember: You never order the larger faeries to do anything—like humans, they resent being ordered about.

Most adult humans may not believe in faeries, but faeries believe in us. In chapters 2 and 3, I will give you information and instructions on how to regain your belief in faeries and call upon their powerful magick to help you in your life. But for now, all I ask is that you keep an open mind to new knowledge. You will be surprised at what you will learn.

Someone once said, "Some things must be believed to be seen." That is exactly how it is with faeries.

Chapter 2

How to Find Faeries and Befriend Them

Everywhere there is a plant, a tree, a weed, even a cactus, there is a faery. The Small Folk, the little winged faeries, are responsible for taking care of every form of vegetation on the face of this earth. If you can grow indoor potted plants of any kind, you have faeries in your house. If you have a vegetable garden or plant flowers in your yard, you have the company of faeries every day. They will actively tend their chosen plants during the growing seasons, and during the dormant season they sleep in or near those plants. Sometimes you will be blessed by these faeries sharing your home off and on during the dark seasons when their plants rest.

If you have indoor plants year-round, but either don't really care about them or tend them in a haphazard manner, their faeries will not be very friendly toward you. It is also unlikely that you will see them. Faeries are highly sensitive to human emotions toward nature and plants. If you do care for your indoor plants, you are a step closer on the path to making faery friends easily.

If you are fortunate enough to spend much time outdoors—in groves of trees, in the forests, along the ocean cliffs, or in the mountains—you may discover the human-size Fay. The Fay live everywhere, except in large cities, and are much more difficult to befriend than the Small Folk.

Since there are two main types of faeries, you will need to find and befriend them according to their type. The easiest ones to befriend are the small winged ones, the Small Folk, for they are more numerous and spend most of their existence in this world.

All faeries appear to have wings, but only some of the Small Folk have actual wings. On the others, what you believe are wings are simply a gathering of magickal energy and power that enables faeries to move quickly from one place to another, or from the physical realm back to the astral realm.

Faery helpers are quite useful when working to improve yourself, your immediate area, or certain spots out in nature. They can also teach you more about music, dancing, and healing than you thought possible. They are experts on flora, fauna, the elements, and the earth itself.

Faeries are sometimes mistaken for guardian angels or spiritual guides, but they are of an entirely different species of astral beings than these helpers. However, if faeries attach themselves to a person or family, they can become both guardians and guides. It is a rare gift and honor to have faery guardians and guides, because most faeries treat humans with deserved suspicion, having found us to be untrustworthy in the past and present.

As with humans, there are good and bad faeries. Some of the faery kin, described in chapter 13, can be very dangerous. However, most of the Fay and the Small Folk are sympathetic to humans who want to learn about them and gain useful ancient knowledge.

Again, you are most likely to find and see faeries, particularly the Small Folk, at dawn, noon, dusk, and midnight. The energies of the earth change at these times, thus opening wider the gateways to the Otherworld realms. Faeries do not especially need these gates to travel from Faery Land, but they are seen in greater numbers at these hours.

The idea of the existence of Faery Land is not as improbable as it first seems. Everyone knows we live in a three-dimensional world. However, Einstein and many other scientists have talked about a fourth dimension that humans may contact or even visit under special circumstances. Psychics have always known that astral travel and deep meditation are two methods of reaching this Otherworld, one part of which is Faery Land. When we reach this fourth dimension, or Otherworld, we find ourselves in another three-dimensional world. In fact, the fourth dimension consists of many other three-dimensional worlds. Therefore, Faery Land and the Otherworld are full of possibilities for exploration and learning.

The Faery World intermingles with this world but lies within another dimension of time and space. Therefore, faeries are not bound by our material or physical laws. Gates into their realm are traditionally connected with water, earth mounds or mountains, caves, or gardens. Gates may also unknowingly be set on or across a line of earth power.

The imaginations and minds of children are the most open, so faeries appear to them easily and often. Adults must open their minds in a childlike manner, with no preconceived ideas, in order to contact the beings from Faery Land.

You never know how one of the Small Folk may present itself to you, as they frequently appear in disguise, especially during the first few meetings. To find faeries, you must look not only with your physical eyes but with your feelings and heart. They may disguise themselves as flowers, birds, or butterflies. Or they may appear riding nearly hidden on cats, dogs, birds, or dragonflies. If you blow bubbles, they may decide to float inside one of the bubbles. They like to curl up in a

The first step in finding faeries and befriending them is to believe in them and to be gentle with the earth. Some things must be believed to be seen, and faeries are one of them.

flower for a nap. Even your favorite ring or piece of jewelry may be the temporary, or permanent, home for a very small faery.

Since the Small Folk love and work with nature, they travel long distances when there is a need to help nature in another part of the world. They have no problem at all with traveling. Therefore, you may find a frivolous, flighty milkweed thistle faery from China in your area or a djinn from Arabia, if there is a need, or if you call to them.

One of the best ways to contact faeries is to sharpen your intuitive senses. Another method is to befriend the loosely connected subspecies of beings called elementals. These beings are connected to and operate within only one element: either earth, air, fire, or water. Nothing can happen within nature unless the elemental needed does its work. The winged Small Folk work with the elements of earth, air, and water, all vital components with which they build the earthly manifestation of all vegetation. Each subset of faery is responsible for a certain type of flower, plant, or tree. Although faeries interact infrequently with the element of fire, the smaller ones do love to dance in candle flames, thus drawing in physical and spiritual energy from this element.

Inside your home, it is not only good feng shui but a great help to faeries, if you place mirrors near sharp corners or beams. These construction details are obstacles for faeries trying to exit a room, but a mirror provides a doorway or portal for them.

It is rare for the Fay to make their presence know to people living in large cities, for two reasons. First, all faeries must have areas of green nature to keep from becoming sick or weak. Large areas of concrete and asphalt and buildings made of unnatural materials do not attract faeries or encourage them to visit, except in times of emergency. Sometimes there is an oasis of greenery and water within a city, which may contain a small colony of faeries or elves.

Second, few city-dwellers are mindful of nature or open to the belief that faeries exist. Faeries do not waste their time and energy trying to work with humans who believe the faeries are merely old superstitions and who do not have the inclination and patience to learn ancient faery knowledge.

If you can have an open mind about faeries and their existence in this world and in Faery Land, then you are ready to begin contacting them.

Start by sitting quietly in a garden or a park, or under a tree. Tune out all the human noises and ordinary nature sounds, until you begin to hear the smallest of noises and then the silence itself. When you reach this state, mentally send out a welcome to the faeries. Their answer will come in the feeling of a very light brush against your body, like a cobweb floating in the breeze. You may have to try this several times before you recognize their answer to your friendship call. When this happens, you are ready to go into a meditation to make a stronger connection with this special species of beings.

Western meditation is very different from Eastern meditation, in which centers on trying to keep all thoughts out of your mind. Westerners have an easier time meditating when they direct the mind in a way to go instead of trying to blank out everything. A meditation written in this style can easily be read into a tape recorder and played back each time you want to do it. After practicing for a while, you will find that you are no longer rigidly following the recorded meditation but are beginning to have experiences that are not on the tape at all.

It is also an excellent idea to have handy a notebook or journal so you can write down your experiences as soon as you return from meditation. Many times you will later remember incidents that you can add to your thoughts following any particular meditation.

To begin any meditation, select a comfortable chair in a room where you will not be disturbed by the telephone, animals, or other people. Sit relaxed but straight in the chair with your hands in your lap.

If you find it helpful, you can record the following instructions onto the tape before you record the meditation: "Breathe slowly and deeply several times, while visualizing a white light that surrounds and interpenetrates your entire body. Feel your muscles relax, especially in your shoulders, neck, and jaw. Do not attempt to analyze whether you are totally relaxed, but simply know you will be. Now begin your mediation."

Meeting Fairies Meditation

Visualize, or think, of yourself standing before a great crystal door with silver hinges and handles. The door is divided down the middle into two leaves. The crystal itself is both milky and clear, revealing only indistinct images and colors behind it. Bright green ivy grows all around it, with strands hanging down over the door in places. Tall stems of blooming foxgloves stand like sentinels at each side of the doorway.

The two leaves of the door slowly start to open, giving you a clear view of a beautiful stretch of flowers backed by tall green trees. Near the grove of trees is a tiny stream bubbling over colorful rocks. Standing in the shadows of the trees are several human-size figures. These are the Fay, who wait to see how you will react.

Small Folk are fluttering around the edges of the door, beckoning and calling for you to enter Faery Land. Several of them fly up to you, tugging at your hair and clothing, urging you to follow them.

You notice there are various sizes of the Small Folk but none larger than about six inches tall. They are also dressed in different styles of clothes, some of which appears to be made of cobweb silk and flower petals, with tiny pieces of moss as decoration.

You enter and begin to wander along tiny paths among the flowers. Butterflies are feeding on the blossoms. Hummingbirds dart in and out of coral bells and trumpet vine flowers. Faeries fly close to you, some riding birds and laughing. Two butterflies hover before your face, then swiftly change into tiny faeries. They seem intent on showing you how they can shape-shift into other forms.

As you look up at the shadowy grove of trees, you see several elegantly dressed faeries coming quickly toward you. They are mounted on very small white horses, their manes decorated with bells and ribbons. These faeries introduce themselves as the kings and queens of various clans of the Small Folk. Each one wears a small crown and tiny jewelry made of gemstones and silver or gold. The queens are dressed in long silk dresses of different colors and a medieval-style cut, with long mantles hanging from their shoulders and down onto their horses. Their feet are clad in elegant dancing slippers. The kings wear full-sleeved shirts gathered at the wrists, doublets, and tight hose fitted into low boots. Small swords and daggers hang at their belts. Courtiers surround them and watch you with interest.

The kings and queens introduce themselves and welcome you to Faery Land. They invite you to join one of their celebrations, assuring you that partaking of their food will not trap you in Faery Land. One queen raises her hand, in which she holds a small wand. The sun quickly sinks behind the mountains to the west, while a bright full moon rises in the east.

All the faeries gather together and lead you down another path until they reach a tall, wide mound of earth. When you reach the top, you see a huge circle of dark green grass edged with thousands of little mushrooms. Many faery thrones line the inner edge of this circle. The kings and queens sit on these thrones, while the courtiers lead away the white horses. The faery royalty invite you to sit on the grass beside them and enjoy the festivities.

Harpers and pipers dressed in various shades of forest green gather in the center of the circle along with faery maidens wearing long brightly colored dresses. As the harpers play their harps and the pipes their bagpipes, the maidens begin to sing wonderful faery songs. You find yourself caught up in the beauty of the singing and melodies.

While drummers join the other musicians, courtiers bring a nectar drink in goblets to everyone in the circle. Yours is larger than the others. As you carefully sip at the nectar, you find it is very pleasant. This is followed by bowls of wild strawberries and pieces of faery cake coated in mushroom butter.

While you are enjoying this unexpected meal, the music begins again, only this time in a lively dance tune. Faeries begin dancing in the air all around the circle. They never cross its boundaries, even in flight, but twist and turn and glide as if they were on the finest dance floor. Small faery children play on the dark green grass around you with tiny white puppies that have red ears. Several small fluffy white cats with red tips on their tails stroll by, their silvery eyes watching everything.

Suddenly one of the queens waves her wand in your direction, and you feel very light, as if you could fly. You think about dancing in the air, and you find yourself floating upward to join the dancers. You twist, glide, and turn with joy as you dance with the Small Folk. You feel your life burdens lifting from your spirit and your heart filling with happiness.

Exhausted and thirsty, you float back to where you were sitting, smile your thanks to the queen who gave you the temporary ability to dance on air, and drink from your goblet of nectar.

Several faery wizards come to talk to you. They answer many of your questions and ask you if you now believe in faeries. They promise to contact you in the future if you say Yes.

You notice that the full moon is almost to the western mountains and there is a soft glow of the rising sun in the east. One of the tall Fay comes out of the forest and beckons to you.

"You must be back through the gates before cock crow," he says.

You turn to find all the Small Folk gone from the green circle.

"Come," the Fay says, as he touches your shoulder and points at the distant gate.

In the blink of an eye, you stand before the open gates and quickly pass through just as the sun floods the sky with light. The doorway behind you closes with a sigh and a click as if a lock has turned.

You immediately think of your physical body and find yourself back in your mediation chair. You are alert, feeling healthy and happy.

Just after this meditation, write down all you can remember of your Faery Land visit. You will remember more things later that you can add to your journal of Faery Land travels. You may also record any opinions on what happened or what you would like to see and experience in another meditation.

There is a long tradition that one can see faeries by performing certain little rituals. The best times for faery rituals, of course, are at dawn, noon, dusk, and midnight, particularly if the moon is full. However, you must be certain that you have no iron on you; as I've said, iron repels faeries.

One method for seeing faeries is to find a stone with a naturally bored hole in it. These can often be found along certain areas of the seashores. If you are fortunate, you can find a naturally bored piece of sandstone to buy. Looking through the hole in the stone will reveal any faeries who may be present.

Faery Elixir Potion

An ancient potion to help you see faeries is easy to make. During a full moon, gather fern seed, a vervain bud, a marigold bud, and a hollyhock bud. Lightly crush these together in a mortar and add a small vial of spring water. Add the flowers and water to a slightly larger bottle of cold-pressed almond oil. Leave this mixture in a warm, dark place for two weeks. Filter the mixture through a coffee filter and pour into a clean bottle.

To find faeries, either look through the bottle of faery elixir, or put a tiny drop on each eyelid, at one of the four appropriate times of day. If you open your mind to the faeries, you should be able to see their fleeting movements or hear their whispering voices on the wind.

You can also stand within a dark green or mushroom-surrounded faery ring at dusk or midnight and dab your eyelids with the seeing mixture. This will help you to see and communicate with the faeries and elves. If you dance in this natural faery circle at these times, watch carefully for an elf or faery. If you see one, say: "Please stop and grant my wish!" Legend says the wish must be granted. Leave a thank-you offering of a flower or small crystal.

To attract faeries into your home, make certain your house is tidy. Faeries do not like dirty houses or chaotic conditions. Another way to make faery friends is to make a small grotto or cave, either inside or outside in the garden. Place small crystals and other stones inside for decoration.

Flower garlands, real or artificial, hung by your main doorway signal to faeries that they are welcome there. So do carefully tended gardens that contain plants known for their strong connection with faeries.

The little house faeries are appreciative of a small bowl of clean water left out at night. They use this water to wash their babies. If you leave out a small feast offering of milk, honey, and cookies or fresh bread, do not expect it to disappear. Faeries drain the nutritional essence from the food instead of actually eating it. Another belief says they take the shadow of the food, which again would remove all nutritional value. Dispose of the offering the next morning.

Sometimes, for whatever reason, you may find your house infested with one or more of the undesirable types of faeries or their kin. If this happens, lightly sprinkle salt in the corners of every room while carrying a stick of burning frankincense incense. Work your way through the house to the main door. When you reach the door, open it and say: "All negatives out! All positives in!" Then quickly close the door.

Some people believe that ringing a bell throughout the house will drive out negative faeries. Churches originally had bells that were rung to discourage the faeries

If one of the trickster faeries should speak to you, be sure to have the last word in the conversation. And say it in rhyme! This will put you in control. One of the most seemingly innocent phrases used by these tricksters is, "How are you today?" You should answer, "I'm fine today, and I'm on my way." Then leave as quickly as possible.

from the area in which the bells could be heard. However, I think it was the loudness of the church bells, rather than the bells themselves, that repelled the faeries; they love to have small bells on their clothing and horse harnesses.

To repel negative faeries and spirits, you can also make a cross out of twigs of oak, ash, and hawthorn and tie it with red thread or yarn. Hang it over the front door.

If you encounter one of the unfriendly faeries elsewhere, an acorn in your pocket will repel them. If you carry a four-leaf clover, that will prevent them from putting a faery glamour, or spell, on you.

If you encounter such negative faeries during a meditation, and they follow you even though you answer in rhyme, there is one thing you can do to stop them. Visualize a short piece of knotted string in your hand. Throw this string at your heckler and move away as fast as you can while the trickster faery tries to figure out the significance of the knotted string.

Even ordinary faeries will sometimes try to trick you, just to see how much you know about them. If one should offer you something, never take the first thing offered. That will put you in their debt. And always offer something in return, even if it is just a leaf, flower, or stone.

When the Faeries Find You

All faeries, but especially the Irish ones, are famous for their white horses. They decorate the horses with sparkling jewels, gold bridles, silver horseshoes, and tiny harps and bells hung in the manes. They ride these magnificent animals during their hunts and on their famous seasonal Faery Rides or Cavalcades.

A few humans have even gone for rides on faery horses but not always to their advantage. They may find themselves unable to dismount; then they must endure a wild, frightening race across country before they are unceremoniously dumped onto the ground. The only time the ride goes well is if a faery or elf invites you to join him or her on horseback. At one time, however, even this invitation was chancy. The human could be kidnapped and taken into Faery Land.

The Irish called Faery Land *Tir-na-Nog,* or "Land of the Young." The orthodox church tried to change the meaning of this name to "Land of the Dead," but couldn't keep the people from believing in faeries. Tir-na-Nog is a place in the west across the sea. The Irish faery horses can run across the waves, so this was no deterrent to going from Tir-na-Nog to Ireland. Tir-na-Nog always remained in the season of spring. The faeries hold constant revelries of dancing, singing, riding out on hunts, and playing games all day. One of their favorite games is hurling, which is still the national sport of Ireland.

Befriending the Pixies

Don't ever ask a pixie for directions if you get lost! This tricksy faery loves to give wrong directions to travelers. Wherever the red-haired pixies go, they leave a tiny, sparkling trail of golden pixie dust—a trail that can be seen only if the sun or moonlight hits it just right. Pixies also have the ability to shape-shift into human size. So if you meet a red-headed man or woman with freckles and eyes full of mischief, you had best beware. This person could be a pixie in disguise.

But if you have a fireplace or wood-burning stove that sits on a hearth, you have the perfect place to host a pixie ball and befriend these mischievous faeries. Sweep the hearth clean and decorate it with flowers. Also, leave out a little milk with a piece of bread and butter. Include a bowl of fresh water for washing their babies.

When you are finished, say aloud: "Come, you pixies, one and all, for I have made a place for your pixie ball."

Then go to bed and listen carefully for the faint sounds of pixie music, for it will surely infiltrate your dreams, if nothing else.

Befriending the Brownies

Brownies originated in the cold Scottish Highlands but immigrated to other parts of the world along with the Scottish people. Their favorite haunts have always been castle ruins, streams, groves of trees, lakes, and rocky seashores—and they'll also take up residence in homes of certain humans they like. Music is one of their greatest talents, so if brownies live with or near you, it is not unusual to hear the faint sound of the pipes on a moonlit night.

To befriend a brownie and attract him into your house, pour a little cream over a stone near his living place. Also, put out a Scottish cake, or bannock, spread with a little honey.

Befriending the Djinn

In the Arabian countries are found the djinn, which we call genies. An entire chapter of the Muslim sacred book, the Koran, is devoted to the djinn and tells how they were created from smokeless fire. The djinn are some of the most powerful faeries in the world. They live in or near caves, wells, or cisterns, which form an entrance to their world. Traditionally, their world lies in the seventh layer of the earth. Although the djinn are huge in size, with knotted hair and giant teeth, they can shape-shift into the form of humans, animals (particularly black cats and dogs), or birds.

If you suspect you are with a djinn, you can ask: "Are you *ins* [human], or are you djinn?" He must answer truthfully. You can make him return to his original form by lighting a candle.

To befriend a djinn, give him a piece of gum or offer to comb out his hair and wind it into a huge knot on top of his head. Such kindness will make him your permanent ally.

If you are clean, neat, and polite, you stand a good chance of impressing a djinn. This will make you very lucky indeed, for this faery frequently grants wishes to his human friends.

The djinn are master craftsmen in using gold and other precious metals to make the most fantastic jewelry. No human has ever been able to copy their intricate, delicate designs. Using their magick, the djinn can also charm horses so that storms follow them when ridden, and they can create the most wonderful enchanted wands. Although extremely powerful, the djinn are not very intelligent in everyday things and frequently misplace their valuables.

Befriending Faeries Around the World

You can find faeries anywhere in the world. Most are natives; there are also European faeries who immigrated to countries around the world along with human explorers, pioneers, and those who decided to settle in far climes. Stowaway faeries joined their European cultural group on the great oceangoing ships by hiding in luggage or shoes, or tucking themselves into shirt pockets.

Faeries of various kinds are found across the Pacific Islands. They have lived in Polynesia for thousands of years, as good friends with their human neighbors. You'll find the Bonita Maidens in the Sullivan Islands. These beautiful water faeries, who dress in seashells, help fishermen find their lost hooks. The Maoris in New Zealand learned to use a fishing net called a *kupenga* by watching the *ponaturi,* or Sea Faeries.

The island of Australia is home to many types of faeries. The original faeries known to the Aboriginal people control the weather and can predict the future. The other faeries followed the European and Asiatic settlers who moved there.

On Hawaii, the faeries are called the *menehune.* They live in volcanoes, where they create fantastic palaces out of lava rock. They also hide out in hollow logs, caves, and in the forested mountains. If you see a small faery there with earthy red skin and bushy eyebrows, you have seen a *menehune.* The faery men have long beards that drag along behind them. The *menehune* love to play and have fun. Some of their favorite pastimes are flying kites, wrestling, diving off cliffs, spinning tops, and racing bamboo sleds down steep, rocky mountainsides. To make friends with them, leave them a gift of a flower or shell necklace.

The *gianes* are found in Italy, where they live in the woods and always carry small spinning wheels with them. They can see the future in the whirling wheels. On the island of Sicily, however, the faeries are called the *folletti*. They are in charge of weather changes. They like nothing better than to whip up a good storm so they can ride on the howling gale. For relaxation, they play a game similar to polo while riding grasshoppers. They like offerings of olives covered with a little olive oil.

The faeries of the Netherlands are so light in body that they are almost invisible. They love to travel through the air, riding inside bubbles. They can also be seen at night while they dance on night-blooming flowers.

High up in the French Alps are faeries called the *lutins*. They can change into any shape they want, but their favorite form is that of a small white horse. As such, they gallop across the icy mountain peaks, moving from place to place with a tiny flash of light like a firefly.

Off the shores of the Scandinavian countries is the most marvelous faery surprise of all. When the sun begins to set, one may be able to see faery islands that rise during the night.

The faeries in Germany like to keep fire-breathing dragons as pets. Tradition says that most of the German faeries live deep in the enchanted Black Forest. There, the trees come alive at night and walk about. These faeries love primroses because they can use them as keys to open treasure boxes.

Gnomes can be found almost anywhere there are trees and forests. They are small and chubby, but kind to humans and animals who are in need. To attract and befriend them, leave an offering of flowers and a little milk.

The *leshy* came from Russia. Fortunately, not many of them migrated with their human people, as they are not favorable to humans. The *leshy* has blue skin, green eyes, and a beard, with his shoes always on the wrong feet. Like pixies, he maliciously misdirects travelers, often to their doom in water.

The most common Russian faery, however, is the *domovoi,* and they have followed their people to new homes around the world. Although they will disguise themselves as piles of hay or big, shaggy cats, you can hear their whispers if you listen closely. They always make noise to warn you if danger is coming. If you are fortunate to have one live with you, always leave a little water and soap in the tub so they can bathe. The only time you might have trouble with the *domovoi* is in March. During this month, they shed their winter skin and grow a lighter one for the summer. The itching caused by the skin shedding makes them grumpy. To show them you care, leave out a little bread and milk.

The cultures of India have believed in faeries for thousands of years. These little greenish blue beings hang out around pine trees, and on hot summer nights they dance on moonlit flowers and vines. They will also celebrate with humans on Hindu holy days, such as Diwali and Holi. Their favorite treats are sweet, sugary foods.

The *duendes,* now common throughout Latin America and in other places around the world, originally came from Spain. However, they do not look the same in every country. In Argentina they are covered with polka dots; in Costa Rica they wear berets and have pointed ears. South American faeries usually live in pristine, isolated areas. However, you may be fortunate enough to find one guarding a single tree. Children see them clearly, but adults have a harder time. They can disguise themselves as almost anything: a whirlwind, shadow, spider, stick, coconut, bird, dog, or cat. Spanish faeries all around the world love offerings of olives.

The faeries on the island of Bermuda are actually shy dwarves who appear as little red-haired apes. Their footprints are very distinctive because the feet point backwards and the big toe sticks out to the side. It is easy to befriend these dwarves, for they love exotic fruits and nuts.

The Mexican faeries, called *aires,* are more like pixies in their mischievous behavior toward humans. Their body forms are made entirely of glistening water. Most of the time they live quietly at the bottom of pools, waterfalls, and rivers, where they cannot be seen by humans. However, when they decide to annoy humans, they gather barrels of clouds, rain, snow, hail, lightning, and thunder, which they dump on unsuspecting humans. They are anything but quiet when they fight amongst themselves; this action produces severe storms.

A Party for Faeries

Faeries around the world are as different from each other as humans are. But everyone, human and faery alike, loves a party. To befriend your resident faeries and to attract more to your home, garden, and/or yard, give a faery party. If you have friends who believe in faeries, invite them also. Send out invitations that include the phrase "in honor of faeries." Be sure to leave an invitation set out in your house and, if possible, somewhere among your flowers or plants.

Prepare a cake or cupcakes with flower designs. Fill vases with flowers and greenery. Fix fruit juice or jasmine tea for everyone to drink. And be certain to have dishes, place settings, and small gifts for everyone, including one for the faeries themselves. Put a small mirror by the faeries' place, because faeries love to look at their reflections.

Buy several small-capped jars and gold or colored glitter at a craft store to make up little gift jars of faery dust. Make your house look like a faery palace with balloons, streamers, confetti, and pictures of faeries. Play music that reminds you of faeries, so everyone's mind will be faery-centered for the party. Decorate each other with face paints and a little glitter. Do impromptu dancing and enjoy yourself. The faeries certainly will. And they will know they are welcome in your home and around you.

You may be surprised at what you see during this party. Napkins and favors may move slightly on the table. The balloons might wobble suddenly without a draft. The flowers in the vases may tilt or bend slightly as an invisible faery settles down for a nap.

Now that you have given a physical party for the faeries of your area, you should think about doing a meditation to visit a faery home. Before you do this meditation, mentally ask permission to be a visitor so the faery family will expect you. The home you will visit will be one belonging to the Small Folk. You will visit the larger Fay later in the book. Begin your meditation with the relaxation techniques described earlier. As with all meditations in this book, you can read the following visualization into a tape recorder so you can fully relax and follow along with the meditation.

Meditation: Visiting a Faery Home

Visualize yourself at the edge of a small, sunny meadow filled with a great variety of blooming flowers. A tiny path wanders across the meadow to three very old oak trees in the meadow's center. You follow the path until you are standing in the shade of the oak trees.

A butterfly flutters before your face, changing into a faery in the blink of an eye. The tiny faery man taps your forehead with his wand three times. You feel yourself shrinking quickly until you are the size of one of the Small Folk. All around you the tall flowers and grass stems are like large shrubs. A grasshopper, the size of a Labrador retriever, bounces across your path, then quickly hops away.

"You are here at last," the faery man says as he flies down to stand beside you. "My family is waiting to meet you. And the wife will be upset if we are late for dinner."

With a smile and a motion of his hand, the faery leads you down a path through the grass and flowers until you reach the big roots of the oldest and biggest oak of all. There, settled against one of the huge arched roots, is a two-story faery house. The sides are covered with the wooden petals from pinecones; the roof is fashioned of strips of bark covered with moss. A small lawn of low, bright green moss grows before the front door.

"Tulip, we're here," the faery man calls as he opens the door and motions for you to come inside. "My name is Acorn," he tells you. "My family and I care for this area around the three ancient oaks. Of course, there are others helping."

Acorn leads the way to the dining room where his wife, Tulip, sits, smiling, at the table.

You notice that the interior of the house is as roughly finished as the outside. The few pieces of furniture are partially hollowed-out old pinecones for chairs, dry oak twigs for the table, and woven grass stems for rugs.

"Have a cup of wildflower tea." Tulip hands you a cup made from an acorn cap. "And do try the seed cakes. They are quite good."

You sit on the pinecone chair, sipping the flavorful tea and talking with the Small Folk.

"You don't really live in this house all the time, do you?" you ask.

Acorn smiles and shakes his head. "All the faeries of this area built it so you would feel comfortable when visiting us. We live out in the fields or up in the oak trees until winter. Then we sleep in warm, cozy tunnels, deep under the tree roots."

Tulip adds, "But all faeries appreciate it when humans make us welcome within their homes for the cold seasons. Some even build special little homes for us to use."

Acorn and Tulip lead you back outside into the dappled sunlight that comes through the leaves of the massive oaks.

"Look about you," Acorn says. "There are faeries everywhere, going about their work and playing among the grasses and flowers."

You look around, but all you see are quick, darting movements that never stay still long enough for you to identify. You keep turning, trying to bring the faeries into focus.

"Oh, no, no," Tulip laughs as she grabs your arm. "Stand still and squint your eyes. If that doesn't work, curl one hand into a tunnel, open at both ends. Then look through the tunnel."

You try both ways until you choose the one that works best for you. You are amazed to see faeries all around you. Some are flying from wildflower to wildflower, singing their flower songs to tell the plants they are loved. Smaller faeries are playing hide-and-seek among the stems of the tall grass. Others are winding cobweb silk, like yarn, onto little wooden frames.

"That is for making clothing," Tulip explains. You suddenly realize you don't need to squint or use your hand anymore to see the faeries, and she smiles. "Once your mind is attuned to Faery Land and faeries, you can see us as easily as you can see yourself in a mirror."

You climb up onto a tree root where you can see better. You see faeries flying around the oak trees, near every plant in the area. In the center of the small meadow, a swarm of faeries hovers over some red and yellow flowers.

"Those are why I am here," Tulip calls up to you.

You climb back down the root to walk with her and hear her story as she leads the way toward the bright flowers.

"Long ago, humans built a home here, but it grew old and fell apart in time. The farmer tore down the old house and built another home far away. However, he made his wife leave behind some of her tulips and daffodils. As custodian of the tulips, I stayed behind with them."

You tilt back your head to see the tall flowers around you. Their scent fills the air, and faery wings send it floating off on a tiny breeze. More and more faeries gather around you until you are encircled by the Small Folk. They begin to dance in a clockwise circle around you, faster and faster, laughing as they dance until the circle is only a blur.

You feel yourself swiftly moving down a twisting tunnel of pink light. "Goodbye," shouts Acorn. You realize that the faeries tricked you, as they have tricked many a human.

When you stop moving, you find yourself inside your physical body once more. You open your eyes to find yourself completely back in the physical world.

Now is a good time to write down all the things the Small Folk told you that could be of use in future communications with them.

When looking for the Small Folk, you have to look with your inner eye as well as your outer ones. Faeries frequently curl up on flower petals to sleep, roll themselves into leaves if it is rainy, or take the form of butterflies, ladybugs, or dragonflies to trick humans. They like to fly on the backs of birds, lie in the warm fur of your cat or dog, or even use mirrors to leave or enter your house.

You will see more of them gathered together at the solstice and equinox than at any other time. The changes of the seasons are traditionally the times of movement of all the faeries from one place to another. Although some of the old tales say the faeries move to new homes at these times, other stories correctly tell of their Rides (Rades, in Scotland) to celebrations and feasting. These four days of season changes are filled with great power and energy that can be useful to any human magician as well.

If you wish to attract faeries into your home, put a little ginger powder or a piece of ginger root out with the milk and clean water. Faeries love the scents of spices but are particularly attracted to ginger. They also love music, dancing, and singing, so if you even hum or whistle while you go about your chores, faeries will be lured by the sound.

Impromptu dancing under the light of a summer full moon will guarantee the company of faeries, who will dance with you. However, do not ever dance within a faery circle of dark grass or mushrooms. This will disrupt your aura until the next full moon. These circles are reserved for faeries only, who do not care for humans tramping about their dancing grounds.

On the solstice and equinox, you can call a greeting to the faeries by using the following chant. It can be said inside or outdoors. Remember to keep your eyes closed in respect, so the faeries do not think you are spying on their Ride. Your connection with the faeries will be stronger if you hold an appropriate flower for each special day: crocus for Imbolc, daffodil or lily for spring equinox, marigold for Beltane, rose for summer solstice, grass heads or grain for Lunasa, daisy for autumn equinox, sunflower for Samhain, and holly for winter solstice.

Through the power of earth and moon,
The power of magick fills the air.
It draws the path the Fair Folk take
On their horses white, and their clothing fair.
As I stand here on the grass,
I ask your blessing as you pass.

This chant acknowledges the existence of faeries, while your closed eyes show faeries your respect. It will strengthen your communication with both the Fay and the Small Folk, something you should do before trying to open and see through a gate into Faery Land.

While standing there, listen carefully for the faint sounds of bells, bridles clinking, the squeak of leather saddles, and the laughter of the faeries as they move on in their Ride. You may even feel light touches as certain faeries bless you as they go by.

The rituals, spells, and herbal concoctions included in this book are very old ones, first taught to humans thousands of years ago by the Fay. When the Fay discovered I had no access to this ancient knowledge, they taught me themselves. The Fay are very precise teachers, right down to every word in a certain place. At the time I was nearly overwhelmed with this teaching, as they began it during a turbulent time of my life. However, I am glad they persisted and badgered me into first writing down, then learning, every spell and ritual I share in this book. For by sharing this knowledge, perhaps I can help people draw closer to the Faery Folk and reconnect with them as of old. Faeries and humans need each other for survival and growth.

Call Within a Faery Circle

This is best done on a full moon but can be done at other times. If you are fortunate enough to have a natural faery ring in your yard, you can use it. If not, form an outline of a circle with small stones. White granite or marble chips are excellent for this, for one can see them in the dark.

Place a piece of raw ginger root in the center of a small plate and surround it with alternating seasonal flowers and tree leaves, especially leaves from the oak, ash, and hawthorn.

Wash carefully and dress in clean clothes. Wait until dusk or midnight, whichever is more convenient for you. Walk to the edge of the circle, carrying the plate of offerings. When you reach the edge of the ring, stop and say: "I ask permission of the Good Folk to enter this circle."

When you feel a comforting welcome, step inside the circle. Stand in the middle of the circle and place the offering dish on the ground in front of you. Say the following chant, though some of the words will not make sense to you. The chant comes from so far in the past that I suspect it contains words foreign to any language known today.

> Nib and Nob, Hib and Hob,
> I call the Good Folk here this day.
> *Azweeth acoon, Eera klamis aroom,*
> Let us be friends 'fore break of day.
> The Veil of Worlds I wish to part,
> and stand beside you, heart to heart.
> *Moor tag su Son, Beetu le Cron,*
> I bring you offering for this request.
> *Meerta feera cloon, Han ma rune,*
> I provide the food for your feast.
> Join me in this circle, wild and free,
> that I might know you and thee know me.
> No harm I bring, nor evil cast.
> I seek your knowledge of the past.
> *Ba su lock tee,*
> I wish to join your company.

Sit down in the circle and wait for the Faery Folk to make themselves known. You may see darting shadows or tiny lights, or feel sudden breezes kiss your body. These are some of the signs that the faeries have accepted your offer of friendship. Sometimes if you half close your eyes, looking through your lashes, it makes it easier to catch glimpses of the Small Folk and the Fay.

Listen with your mind and outer ears for melodic music that floats in and out of your hearing. If you are fortunate enough to receive a gift at this first meeting, it will likely be a small black stone that appears before you, or a leaf that floats on the air, settling inside the circle.

Stand and hold out your arms in front of you, over the plate of plants and leaves, and say, "I thank you for your friendship free. So feast and make merry."

Turn and step outside the circle, not looking back. Leave the plate until the next morning. Although the offering will remain, the energy of the plants and leaves will be gone. Put the remains in your compost bin or garden.

If the Faery Folk did not give you a gift the night of the Call, keep alert, for a gift of nature will be given to you soon.

Using a Holey Stone

A true holey stone is a stone with a naturally bored hole through it. You can find them along beaches and occasionally discover them for sale in shops. Never accept a stone with a man-bored hole through it; it will not work the same way the true holey stone does.

Most people are aware that the holey stone is used to see faeries. However, few know that you can use it to look into the past or the future.

To see into the past, stand on one leg, close your right eye, and squint through the hole with your left eye. To see into the future, reverse the process: Close your left eye and look with your right. Like using a magick mirror or crystal ball, this technique requires much practice.

When you use the holey stone to see faeries, you are using it more as a tunnel-shaped telescope. This works best at dawn, dusk, and midnight. You can use either eye but must close the other. Before you start, say the following chant:

> Faery Folk, all wild and free,
> Let me your true shape see.

Holding the holey stone to one eye, look through it for quick movements, darting lights, flitting shadows. It may take you some time to see color through the stone. Slowly turn and look to the right through the stone. Repeat the process, looking to your left through the stone. Gently and slowly turning in a circle, look all around you. Be sure to also look up and down, not all at one level. The Small Folk love to tease and may flitter above or below your line of sight. One time, they covered the hole in my holey stone as a joke.

If they persist in keeping out of sight, entice them with something fun, for the Small Folk love to have fun:

> Come join me in fun and travel fast,
> that we may soar on dandelion flowers.
> Waving at the birds as we pass,
> and forgetful of both time and hours.
> For in the night your powers expand,
> and festivals and dancing occur.
> With your lovely queen leading your band,
> all earthly sensations blur.
> I await your presence night and day,
> and hope to see you at your play.

As with all things to do with faeries, one must have patience. Their vibrational rate is higher than ours, which makes them invisible most of the time. Sitting quietly and relaxing raises your vibrations so there's less difference for the faeries to bridge to reach you.

Chapter 3

Opening the Door to the Faery World

Opening the door to Faery Land is primarily a matter of making a mental change of attitude, it happens on the subconscious level rather than a physical one. Today, it is extremely unusual for a human to cross into Faery Land with the physical body as they did centuries ago. The faeries seem to have erected a protection against this. Perhaps they grew tired of humans invading their territory, unannounced and unwanted. However, you can sometimes see through a doorway into Faery Land—a realm that looks much like this one but is slightly different. Or, you may accidentally wander into the very outer edges of Faery Land, where everything you see takes on a more vibrant life.

The best times to attempt to open doorways into Faery Land are on the eight special days. These eight days of the year have the strongest earth energy tides and are the easiest to tap into for use. They are also the best times to catch a glimpse of one or more types of faeries, especially the Small Folk.

These eight days are also the times of the Faery Rides. Both the Fay and the Small Folk travel to certain secret places where they celebrate their spiritual rituals and have feasts and dances, and distant clans meet again. The long lines of faeries on their white horses are visible for short periods of time, while the Faery Cavalcade makes its way from one large portal to another. These processions always follow ancient lines of power deep within the earth, which is why the Rides are seen in the same areas year after year. When entire clans of faeries are moving from one place to another, it is necessary for them to use the larger, more powerful doorways to accommodate their numbers.

If you are fortunate enough to see the Rides, you will find the faeries decked in their finest attire. The king and queen who lead the Ride are always the most splendid and wear crowns.

The other faery women wear long dresses embroidered with silver and gold designs. Satin dancing slippers shod their feet. Decked in jewelry with their hair flowing down their backs, these ladies wear leather gloves to handle their horses' reins. The Fay ladies and men may wear heavy leather gauntlets on which perch falcons. In summer, their capes are as light as cobwebs, floating in the breeze behind them as they ride. In winter, the capes and hoods are lined with fur and thistle down.

The faery men, particularly the courtiers, wear colorful breeches, white shirts with full sleeves gathered at the wrists, embroidered vests and doublets, and shiny black boots that sometimes reach to the knee. Their hair is tied back with satin ribbons; they also wear broad-brimmed hats with feathers stuck in one side of the band. They carry silver daggers and swords slung from their belts. Their capes are not as long as those of the ladies, only brushing their fancy saddles.

Accompanying both the Fay and the Small Folk, one usually sees the Cwn Annwn, the white faery dogs that have red ears and eyes. The Small Folk allow their dogs to range free, but the Fay have their hound masters leash their dogs and follow the animals along the route.

The Faery Doorways

It is very difficult for humans to find natural faery doorways, although they are all around us. Faery Land is a separate world, yet at the same time it is a world that interpenetrates our world. Faeries and humans have a strong affinity, whether they both admit it or not. Faeries need our help to keep the world balanced, and we need theirs. We are inter-connected. Only a thin membrane of astral energy lies between the two worlds, but the membrane has at least seven major doorways that are usable to humans. You cannot force your way into Faery Land, nor can you enter without the right key. Knowing how to prepare the mind for each doorway is the key to passing from this world into Faery Land.

The natural doorways are not on different levels, nor is any particular one better than another. You can choose to walk through any of these doors at any time in your life, depending upon your mood and ability to focus. It's not necessary to enter the doorways in any special order. They become available to you according to the growth in your personal life, which means you may never see some of the doors. Though we know of seven major doorways that are available to humans, you may find others on your journeys. The journey itself becomes the destination, for entering Faery Land is an ongoing process.

You will not find these invisible doorways in a particular place or in a specific order. They appear to the seeker when the seeker is mentally ready to experience what lies beyond the door. However, meditating upon each door in its order helps attract that doorway so you may enter when the faeries deem you ready.

The key to opening these doors, besides your being subconsciously ready, is to shift your consciousness into one of welcome and greeting as a friend. You are not required to be gifted or psychic; you just have to be sincere. When you arrive in Faery Land, you will be both a guest and a student. You will not only observe but you may well be called upon to participate. However, the most important thing for you to do once you are in Faery Land is to project your true friendship to the faeries. Only then will the faeries offer friendship and help to you.

The first doorway is acknowledging the existence of faeries. This is the door by which most children enter, for they have no prejudices or doubts that what they see is real. The key for adults is the admission that you know faeries are there, even though you may not see them. The only way to share the wonders of Faery Land is to slow down, sit quietly, and subtly let your vibrations rise to meet theirs. When your cells begin to vibrate at this higher rate, they resonate more with the faeries, and powerful changes begin psychologically without your being aware of it.

Everything on this planet, even the inanimate, has its own unique presence and expression of the heart, or the individuality of that object. The more you accept and recognize faeries, the more of the real you comes out. The faeries demand your sincere willingness to be present with your true self—the self other people, and even you, may never see or know—before they will reveal their presence to you.

After entering this doorway, you may begin to catch faint glimpses of darting figures in the corners of your eye, or you may see unexplainable pinpoints of light across a semidark room. You have caught the interest of the Small Folk. They will now be watching you to see if you continue to progress.

The second doorway is the one most adults enter first. Everyone who has had contact with nature or plants in any way is already prepared to enter Faery Land, the destination beyond this gate. How deep you enter Faery Land depends upon the affinity you have developed in gently touching flowers and trees. If you can love and admire each separate leaf and petal, you are likely to go farther into Faery Land than those who haven't learned to acknowledge the individuality of each plant and each of its parts. For, by admiring each part, you are expressing love for the faeries who care for that specific plant.

Faeries understand the variety of emotions to which humans are subject. As long as you are sincere and don't harm nature, they will help you overcome feelings of sadness and loneliness by having you embrace a tree for comfort and inspiring your negative emotions to get carried away by the scent of flowers or the sharp, clean smell of the air after a rain. Touching vegetables in your garden will send your anger into the earth to be transformed into positive energy again.

After you successfully enter this doorway, the Small Folk will help you to see faint images of themselves as they move about their business with the plants. A faery may lie curled up in a flower petal, sleeping. You may hear the very faint songs of encouragement and love that faeries sing to the plants in their care. Put your emotions aside and listen deeply.

The third doorway is listening. All humans listen with their outer ears, but few listen with their inner ears and heart. You need to become aware of the universal rhythm that is the foundation of everything, including faeries. They often go beyond their own language to express this universal rhythm through song and dance. Learn to listen with your entire body, especially at dawn and dusk. The smallest sound that you never noticed before can draw you deeper into Faery Land. Soon you will discover that every sound is associated with a different color or shade of color. When you learn this technique, the colors of everything around you will be brighter and clearer than they were before.

At this stage of your seeking, you will learn to hear the songs of colors and the tunes of the auras around everything, even inanimate objects. If you have a healing gift, you will learn to discern between the beauty of another human's healthy aura and that of one who is ill.

The fourth doorway is inner seeing. Here, your physical eyes are of no use to you; to adults, seeing is not necessarily believing. Here, the adage "Some things must be believed to be seen" comes into play. If you are clairvoyant, you should have little trouble with this doorway, unless you have rock-hard beliefs about how faeries should look and act. If you think of faeries as evil, they will appear in evil forms.

As previously stated, faery bodies are composed of higher vibrations than those of humans. Therefore, we most often see them as pulsating spots of light. However, humans have seen faeries in different cultural costumes and appearances for centuries. So here we have evidence that at least the Small Folk, who want to be seen and acknowledged by all humans, will take on the appearance of the strongest faery images in any human mind. They seem to have a need to be seen, and we have a need to see them. But unless you have a deep desire to see the truth of Faery Land, you will have trouble seeing a faery.

When you reach the fourth doorway, you may well see one of the Fay, the human-size faeries. This Fay may have been appointed as a faery teacher to you, or you may have attracted one who wishes to become a friend or lover.

The fifth doorway is where you must surrender to the awe of the diversity of the universe on all its levels. In this state, you will realize the value of simply being. As you progress toward believing that faeries are always present, there will be a subtle shift within your physical body and the vibrations surrounding it. You will sense a good, but tingly, feeling in your solar plexus (stomach) area, or perhaps in your heart, up and down your spine, or in the brain. There is no mistaking this feeling, for you will know you are beginning to let go of old, outdated beliefs and are standing on the threshold of a new, powerful experience.

To get over this threshold of awe, you must let your body and mind resonate with the vibrations of Faery Land. You cannot make the crossing as long as the left (analytical) side of the brain is in control. The right (creative) side of the brain, the part to which anything is possible, must control for you to cross this threshold. The best way to practice for this doorway is to sit on the floor or lie on the earth, eyes closed, with your arms and legs uncrossed. Be silent and listen to your body. Don't try to think of anything. Soon you will be able to tell where your body is most alive. You will feel the beginnings of awe at this discovery. Let the feeling wash over you as you open your eyes.

The last two doorways can be entered only by a human with great understanding and experience in faery techniques. The humans who enter these last gates are usually older people who have known the joys and sorrows of life, and still manage to believe in life and faeries. There are no exercises to make you ready for these doorways, and you must enter them totally alone. A Fay teacher or friend, if you are fortunate enough to have one, will give you courage and advice about entering these doorways.

Door six is knowing the silence and stillness. Absolute knowing is a state that occurs deep within the subconscious mind, a state so powerful and solid that you never question it. At this stage, the seeker of faeries realizes that everything is surrounded by silence and stillness, a kind of magickal aura inside the regular aura. The seeker must be comfortable with the self, without companionship or intimacy, even in the state of vulnerability. This is a person who has moved beyond faith and trust to a state of acceptance of whatever is in life.

You have moved completely beyond the realm of the Small Folk now, and into the Fay realm where you are likely to meet and speak with Fay magicians and healers. The personal instruction and advice you receive from them is tailored specifically for you and your life. They will teach you to weave together the

Things around you will look slightly different. Your mind is beginning to adjust to seeing the world from a faery point of view. By now, you should see more quick, darting move-ments from the corners of your eyes, and/or tiny moving spots of light that may zigzag across a room. You might also see the tall shadow of a Fay standing in the half-light of a room or hallway. Acknowledge their existence and welcome them to your home.

43

powers of the elements to heal others and the planet. You can also use this magickal power for yourself, if used in a selfless manner.

Door seven is sharing the dance of life. This doorway can lead to the deepest parts of Faery Land and to the wisest of all the Fay, the Mystics. Door six was the last doorway where a human had to prove anything. Door seven represents the unconditional giving and receiving between humans and faeries, of great generosity without thought of repayment, compassionate cooperation, a place where there is no hidden agenda on either side. Spiritual love and knowledge are freely exchanged. The human who enters here offers his or her own unique gifts to help the faeries balance all nature and keep the Dance of Life moving. The Dance of Life is the universal rhythm that flows through everything, allowing and aiding its growth and development.

You do not choose to enter this doorway; it chooses you, based on qualities about which we know nothing. If chosen, you suddenly find yourself there. Humans who are allowed to enter this door are unique people who hide nothing and are no longer afraid of others discovering their faults and failures. Many times they have risked their hearts in love of another human, children, friends, family, or a cause, and many times they have lost. However, in the end they are victorious in their goals and satisfied with their lives.

Sooner or later all humans and faeries must enter this last doorway. Deep within our hearts is the desire to learn the secret hidden behind this door: that unconditional, universal love is the ultimate gift one can give to another being, that it is the most healing, creating force in the galaxy.

Sometimes a person will wander into the edges of Faery Land without quite realizing what has happened. This usually occurs at the crossing of energy lines deep within the earth. Where two or more of these lines meet and cross, it creates a strong power point that may radiate out as far as one hundred feet from the center. One cannot find these lines by looking, for nothing physical shows. However, these lines are detectable with a dowsing rod or pendulum. When using these devices, you will have to cross and recross the energy line, marking it as you go, in order to follow its path. For, contrary to what some believe, energy lines are not necessarily straight.

When you come across a power spot, the dowsing rod or pendulum will react in an extreme fashion. A dowsing rod may move up or down so suddenly that it contacts your body in a painful manner (be careful). If you are using a pendulum, the device will begin a fast, clockwise spin until it rotates parallel, or nearly so, to your hand. To determine the circumference of this power spot, slowly step backward one step at a time while closely watching the device in your hand. As the spin or movement lessens, you are getting close to the outer edge of the power spot.

Never stand or sit in the middle of a power spot for more than five minutes at a time. Overstimulation can cause nervousness, stomach or intestinal problems, and headaches. It is much better to work on seeing and meeting faeries at the outer edge of this site. Both you and the faeries will be more comfortable, and the energy there will aid you in seeing faeries.

Another method is to construct a physical gate that will enable you to see into Faery Land. This works particularly well if you have planted a special faery garden or made a bower with a swing-chair. This area will gradually attract faeries and their energy, and will be a good place for you to sit and meditate.

The simplest method is to plant two faery trees with a walkway between them. You can also get two very large planters and set them far enough apart so you can walk between them. Fill them with potting soil and plant flowers that attract faeries. It is best to have a chair or two sitting beside a small patch of flowers on the other side of this "gate."

A more elaborate gate consists of two large wooden planter boxes and a standard trellis. Using screws short enough to not go through the box into the soil, attach the trellis to one planter box, then the other. Move the gateway into the place where you want it to remain. Plant climbing vines, such as honeysuckle and jasmine, in the planting boxes with quality potting soil. Then put a thick layer of white granite or marble chips on the ground between the boxes. You can extend this special pathway a foot or two on each side of the trellis entry.

When you walk over this white path under the archway, you will feel as if you are entering another world. You can tell the difference if you enter your faery area by walking around the trellis instead of under it. The vibrational feeling will not be the same—and you are less likely to have faery experiences.

You can achieve the same effect by using two wide columns on which you might set potted plants. Put the marble chips between the columns to add to the power of entering the outer edges of Faery Land.

The first time you pass through your new gate into the edges of Faery Land, you should chant something similar to the following verse:

> This gate will now open, for I have the key
> Of trust and belief in the Land of Faery.

Simple handmade gates help define in the human mind the line between this world and Faery Land. This makes it much easier to contact faeries. By sitting beyond your gate, you will begin to experience more and clearer dreams. Sudden ideas of inspiration will flash into your mind. You will look at the world around you in a different way, seeing and admiring the simplest of things, such as the way clouds make patterns or the shadow of an object does not remind you of the object itself. It is another way of preparing yourself and your mind to meet and learn from faeries.

Calling Magick from a Faery Summer Moon

Although this ritual will work on any full moon during the summer months, it is strongest on the full moon closest to summer solstice, around June 22 (the date may fluctuate a day or so each year).

You will need a small silver or crystal bowl (silver is best if it is available), half-full of water. You will also need two white candles and one silver candle in holders. Finally, you will need a sink stone (a flat piece of marble or other natural rock) or a piece of magickal jewelry.

Wait until the full moon is high in the sky and can shine its beams down into the bowl of water. Set the bowl where the moonbeams have direct passage into the water. Set the two white candles, one at each side of the bowl, far enough away that you can freely move your arms around the bowl as you work. Set the silver candle at the far side of the bowl from you, thus creating a triangle of the candles. Do not light the candles yet.

Kneel down, facing the bowl, the moon, and the silver candle. If you plan to transfer the magickal energy into a sink stone, have the stone close beside your power hand (right if you are right-handed, left if you are left-handed). Otherwise, wear a piece of magickal jewelry that will collect this potent energy.

Lean forward, blow gently three times on the water in the bowl, and chant:

> Thrice I blow the breath of life upon this clear water.
> Thrice I ask the faery of the moon to answer my plea.
> Thrice I will burn lights of joy and thanks in her honor,
>   That she be my friend and teacher for all eternity.

Hold your arms up toward the moon and chant:

Bloosaw, faery of the moon, *bloosaw.*
I am a mortal wending my way back to the oldest knowledge,
That held and taught by the Faery Folk.
I ask your aid in filling me with your potent power,
That I may learn to use it and understand you better.
Bloosaw, faery of the moon, *bloosaw.*

Gently sweep your cupped hands over the bowl of water toward your heart. Do this until you feel the energy waning. Breathe deeply as you rise to light the three candles. Now place your power hand on the sink stone or the magickal jewelry and chant:

From thee to me.

Repeat this simple chant until you feel that all, or most, of the magickal energy has been transferred.

Kneel again before the bowl. Gaze into the water as if you were looking into a crystal ball. Ask a question that is important to you. The residue of energy remaining in the water may help you to see an answer to your question. The vision may come in the water or in your mind.

Leave the candles to burn for at least half an hour. Take the bowl of water into your hands and say:

From moon to water,
From water to earth.
The circle of all energy is complete.

Pour the water out into your flowers or lawn.

Chapter 4

The Fay

Most people think of faeries as little hominoid creatures with tiny fluttering wings. They have forgotten, or never knew, that there is another type of faery, the one called the Fay. The Fay are human-size faeries; in Celtic areas, the stories are quite specific about this, even though the Fay were respectfully spoken of as the Good Folk or the Wise Old Ones. The Fay are mysterious and elusive because of their caution in contacting and appearing to humans. They are the most intelligent of the Faery Folk and the closest to humans in appearance and body type. Most of the oldest stories about faeries in Europe and the Middle East describe the Fay as one who sometimes had children with human partners or who lured humans into Faery Land for a period of time.

The Faery Folk, in general, are composed of several cultures and subcultures of beings who are all related in some manner. The Fay and the elves are the most intelligent and ingenious members of Faery Land; they are also the ones who hold the keys to much ancient knowledge. The Fay and the elves have wider-reaching powers, activities, and authority.

Their distant cousins, the dwarves, also know lost ancient knowledge but are far less trusting of humans and rarely interact with them.

Some people make the mistake of looking upon the Fay and Small Folk as displaced, ancient cultural deities. Even though the deities have some similar traits and abilities, they are not faeries. The Faery Folk are a species unto themselves. They were never worshipped but were treated with great respect because of their powers.

The small, winged faeries, whom I call the Small Folk, are a sub-species of faery, along with the distantly related elementals and nature spirits. The Small Folk and the others are watched over, taught, and protected by the larger Fay and the elves. The smaller beings usually reside in one place and are connected with one type of energy, and their work in the world is basically limited to one type of activity. A few of the solitary subspecies live entirely alone and are not friendly toward humans at all.

Other astral creatures, such as dragons, gargoyles, and the great winged bulls, are not related to faeries but are species of their own.

The only times the Fay deliberately interact with humans is when an individual firmly believes in their existence and tries to become attuned to nature in some manner. They may also interact with a human who selflessly works in the psychic fields, particularly healing and foretelling.

Although interaction with the Small Folk is joyful and raises the vibrations around you and your home, it is the larger Fay who have the most to teach humans. They are the caretakers of ancient knowledge that has been forgotten on earth—knowledge that could one day heal the earth and all humans who live here, not only of physical ailments but also of the mental, emotional, and spiritual problems to which humans are susceptible.

As in human society, there are different levels of intelligence and ambition among the Fay. However, all of them are attuned to the Goddess and the God, nature, and caring for the earth and the Small Folk.

The Fay have been described as very beautiful beings who have many of the same interests humans do. Tall and slender, Fay men and women easily reach six feet tall or taller. They have slightly pointed ears and sometimes a little upward tilt to the outer corners of their eyes. Although their skin is frequently lightly bronzed or tanned, their skin colors vary as much as those of humans. The colors of their hair and eyes usually mimics the shades found in nature. Their hair color ranges from black to a pale blonde, while their eyes can be many different colors, such as all shades of green, brown, black, and the deepest of blues. Their clothing ranges from quite elegant in the courts and larger clans to rather rustic and delightful in the smaller communities.

Fay from both the Seelie and Unseelie Courts are curious about humans and their actions. On rare occasions, a Fay from the Unseelie Court becomes attracted to a human and changes his or her allegiance because of that human's influence. But the attraction between the Fay and the human must be very powerful for this to happen, so much so that the Fay will choose to change rather than lose the connection with the human. Be wary of all faery lovers who appear to humans, as they are adept at masking their true emotions and intents.

Most Fay do not consider alliances with humans as very important. Permanent attachment with a Fay lover occurs seldom but is very powerful and lasts for the human's lifetime. Children can be born of this union. Most of these children are raised in the Faery Kingdom, but a very few have been known to be born in the human world and

The Fay, and elves in particular, have an ethereal beauty that attracts humans, whether they are seen by chance encounter or deliberately. If a Fay becomes enamored of a certain human, she or he will appear to the human so a relationship can begin. This is not a frequent happening. At the same time, the Fay can be aloof, suspicious, and taciturn until the human who seeks them proves her or his trustworthiness.

stay here. These rare Fay-human children act differently from ordinary human children in that they are more attuned to nature, prefer to spend their time alone, and are very psychic. These children prefer to roam the forests and groves and communicate with animals; they do not adapt easily to human rules.

The laws of the Fay, both Seelie and Unseelie Courts, are more serious than those of the Small Folk. Since the Fay are the guardians and protectors of the Small Folk, they must live a more structured life. However, their first law is the same as that of the smaller faeries: Live in harmony and spirituality with nature, the God, and the Goddess.

Many of their laws are similar to those of humans:

- Do not harm others, including anything in nature, unless it cannot be avoided
- Do not cheat, lie, or steal, for those actions harm all
- Do not initiate contact with humans unless the experience has been thoroughly discussed with the Council of Elders and Masters
- Guard the gates to Faery Land from all invaders who come filled with ill-will and malice
- Do not reveal faery secrets and knowledge to those not worthy
- It is forbidden to be cruel or mistreat wild animals, friendly astral creatures, humans, or each other, especially children

The exception to the rule about mistreating each other occurs during battles between the Seelie and Unseelie Courts. However, these wars are infrequent.

The law concerning treatment of humans is more open to interpretation, because it depends on what the human has done. For example, building a house across a seasonal faery path is justification for harassment and ill luck, as is interfering with faery dances and rituals, unless invited to join in.

The Fay do not have wings; rather, what appears to be wings on their backs near their shoulders is actually a collected pool of energy that enables them to move swiftly from one place to another.

This same physical description fits the faeries' close cousins, the elves. The word Elfame, instead of Faery Land, appeared in Scottish lore after the absorption of the Viking culture and traditions. The word probably should be written Elfhame, meaning Elf Home. It means the same as Faery Land, but the world Elfhame is Scandinavian in origin. The word Summerland, sometimes used to describe Faery Land, came into being with the rise of Victorian Spiritualists and is not traditional at all.

The Scottish Celtic division of the Fay into the Seelie and Unseelie Courts may explain the ambiguity held by other cultures about the safety of faeries, since few cultures made distinctions between types of faeries. Members of the Seelie Court, or Blessed Court, are friendlier toward humans, more likely to help, and known to bestow special psychic gifts to certain people. Members of the Unseelie Court, or Unblessed Court, are not evil faeries; they simply distrust humans to a greater degree, have different rules than the Seelie Court, and are a slightly different cultural group than the others. They also tend to be darker in color. However, they, too, have access to very ancient knowledge and power that can prove valuable to humans. Since members of the Unseelie Court are so suspicious of humans, though, it is far harder to gain their cooperation and friendship.

As with the Seelie and Unseelie Courts among the faeries, Scandinavian legends mention both light and dark elves. The descriptions of the two elf cultures are basically the same as those of the Fay. They are human-size, very intelligent, with a culture that closely matches that of the Fay. The light elves are more apt to associate with humans, helping them as needed. The dark elves stay more to themselves and avoid humans whenever possible, just as members of the Unseelie Court do.

The Fay sometimes draw humans into Faery Land. The humans sometimes go willingly, sometimes unwillingly. They may stay there for days, months, or years, not realizing the passage of time on earth, since time is quite different in Faery Land. There are many stories of Fay kidnapping human men and women to whom they have taken a fancy. Even after they're returned to their homes a few of these humans choose to go back to Faery Land at some point in their lives, as they are no longer comfortable with humans and the earth plane.

An example of a free will journey into Faery Land and the return after a given period of time is found in the poem "Thomas the Rhymer," which is based upon an actual person who lived in thirteenth-century Scotland. In land deeds signed during this period, his name is listed as Thomas Rymour de Ercildoune. He was also known as Lord Learmont and True Thomas.

The tale goes that one day while Thomas played his lute under a tree in the forest, the Queen of Faery Land (some versions say Elfland) rode by on her white horse. She became enamored of Thomas and enticed him to kiss her. After her kiss, Thomas willingly went with the queen into Faery Land, where he stayed for seven years and dressed in faery green. After seven years, the queen returned Thomas to the mortal world, bestowing upon him the gift of a prophetic tongue that could not lie. He became widely famous as a poet and a prophet. He must have married after his return, for the land deeds also list the name of his son.

However, Thomas the Rhymer never forgot Faery Land. In later years, as Thomas, his family, and friends were feasting at his castle, a villager rushed in with the news that a white stag and doe had come out of the deep forests and were moving toward the castle. Thomas knew instantly that he was being called back to Faery Land.

He left the castle and met the white deer; they turned and led him into the forests. No one ever saw Thomas Rymour de Ercildoune on the mortal plane again. Yet many who visit Faery Land have seen him over the years. He helps mortals gain access to faeries who will help with certain needs.

There is the Scottish story of Tam Lin, a lone knight who was kidnapped by the Faery Queen when he fell from his horse. The queen made him guardian of Carterhaugh, a wild place of trees and roses. The clan chief warned every woman to stay away from that area because of the danger from Tam Lin: He would steal their jewelry or their virginity.

However, Janet, daughter of the clan chief, defied the order because her father had given her the area that contained Carterhaugh. She became pregnant with Tam Lin's child. Tam Lin told her to be at Miles Cross on Halloween, when the Faery Troop would pass by, and instructed her how to bring him back into the mortal world again by pulling him from his horse. The Faery Queen, angry at Janet for pulling Tam Lin from his horse, turned the enchanted knight into a variety of dangerous creatures, including a red-hot bar of iron. Janet held onto her love until he turned back into a naked man; she covered him with her green mantle, thus hiding him from the sight of the faeries. Deprived of their human hostage, the Faery Troop rode on, leaving Tam Lin with Janet.

Robert Kirk, a Scottish minister, wrote *The Secret Commonwealth of Elves, Fauns and Fairies* (currently out of print). In this book, he talks of the Second Sight, or the ability to use intuition to see the faeries. He cautions his readers to stay away from known faery mounds, as the earth hills provide a kind of entrance into Faery Land. One could wander in accidentally or be kidnapped if one stood on the mound, particularly at night.

However, Robert Kirk did not follow his own advice. He slept on a local faery mound and disappeared entirely. Just before his pregnant wife gave birth, Kirk appeared to his cousin in a dream. Kirk told the man that he would appear at the child's christening, and if the cousin stabbed his dirk into a certain chair as soon as he appeared, Kirk would be released from Faery Land. The christening day came, and the cousin stood ready with his dirk. However, he was so shocked when Robert Kirk appeared before him that he forgot to stab the chair. And Kirk disappeared back into Faery Land forever.

All of these tales involve human-size faeries, for a faery would have to be large to physically remove a human, willingly or unwillingly, even by magick, into Faery Land.

Although labels and categorization divides the Fay into the Seelie and Unseelie Courts and the elves into light and dark, this does not mean that each type lives in one large group, governed by only one king and one queen. The names mean only that a conglomeration of smaller groups live by the same principles and laws, coming together at their main court only at various seasons of the year or during an emergency. The smaller groups, or clans, each live under a minor king and queen, and all answer to the high king and high queen of their main clan.

There are also a few Fay and elves that live alone or with their mates. This type of Fay is usually one trained to care for and protect certain areas of the earth or to perform specific duties for the Clan. However, just as with humans, some of the Fay and elves simply do not care to live in, or close to, larger groups of their kind.

The two types of Fay, Seelie and Unseelie, do not live together, nor do they associate very much with their counterparts. Even the Fay of each type do not live in communities or towns as we would know them. The living and learning conditions of the two types, however, are very similar. Only some of the rules are different.

For example, the Fay of the Unseelie Court and Dark Elves are more likely to cause problems for humans, than the Fay of the Seelie Court. The Unseelie Court and Dark Elves are more belligerent and vengeful over human trespass or destruction in certain wild areas. They are also the most elusive and difficult to befriend. Only advanced magicians should attempt to contact and work with the Unseelie Court or Dark Elves. One must be very careful.

Since living conditions of the two types of Fay and elves are so similar, an explanation of the Seelie Court will allow the reader to understand the basics of the Unseelie Court as well.

The Seelie Court, where the High King and High Queen have their main residence, is usually a vast, beautiful collection of buildings either along a cliff side or sprawled among several huge trees in a special grove. These buildings, and those of the famous Faery Schools of Learning, are fashioned of natural stones, including much clear crystal, and decorated with waterfalls, pools, streams, vines, and flowers.

In the Schools of Learning, those of the Fay who can pass difficult exams can train for special positions in the faery kingdom. It is only these Fay who communicate with the opposite court or the elves, and they are sometimes sent on special missions to humans. On very rare occasions, members of the opposite court or elves are allowed to study in the other's Schools of Learning.

The majority of family houses are not as elaborate as the court buildings. They are built to blend in with the natural surroundings. Each house reflects the personality of the Fay who live there, just as human houses do. Inside, the furniture is lavishly made of wood and precious metals. The materials of the cushions, blankets, rugs, and tapestries are dyed with natural plant dyes and woven of cotton and

Smaller groups of the Fay have their own dwellings in various groves, near streams and rivers, beside lakes, near waterfalls, on the edge of marshlands, or high in the mountains. Dwellings are situated as near to earth current lines of energy as possible. These currents are either what humans call ley lines or natural underground streams.

wool on looms. Wooden objects are carved with intricate designs and scenes of old tales or places in nature. Much elaborate embroidery decorates clothing, saddle blankets, and interior furnishings.

A Fay male and female may decide to commit to a binding ceremony, similar to a human marriage, but this is not required in Faery Land. They are much more open to a variety of living arrangements than humans are. Fay families tend to have a limited number of children, not close together in age, as the Fay, and faeries in general, live much longer than humans do. Fay children are highly prized, perhaps because there are so few of them.

The two great Schools of Learning in the High Fay Court hold much forgotten knowledge and information never released into the human realm. Similar schools are found in both the Seelie and Unseelie Courts, as well as among the elves. Any Fay, male or female, can apply for a position in either school. However, they cannot gain entrance unless they pass the tests given by the masters and council of elders. The masters and some of the elders are often professors of the schools. Only a small number of students are studying at any given time; it is common for a master or elder to have only two or three students.

The council of elders is primarily composed of the very ancient Fay, although some are much younger. They offer guidance and suggestions to the schoolmasters when called upon. The elders spend most of their time contemplating the needs of the community and the Fay as well as the earth as a whole; they meditate frequently. The masters of the schools are not given the term "master" because of their age or number of years in training. They gain this position because they are absolute masters of their chosen field or craft; their position of master must be confirmed by the council of elders. Masters may retire to the elder community at any time. They are not required to serve any given number of years in the position of teaching master.

The Fay wishing to enter these Schools of Learning are hand-chosen for their inherent abilities, personality, temperament, and commitment. Age seems to have no bearing upon when a Fay is entered into one of these schools, except that the Fay in question must be old enough and intelligent enough to be responsible and emotionally stable if removed from the family setting for long periods of time. It takes years of study and work for these students to become proficient in a particular subject or craft. Each student must work her or his way up from apprentice to academic to adept.

Humans should understand that the Fay who enter these schools do so to learn the highest levels of their chosen craft. Their talents are honed to the greatest degree possible. The work they turn out, whether it be physical or mental, is of great power and beauty, beyond anything humans could ever know or see.

One of these schools is for the instruction of craftspeople, a position highly valued among the Fay, for they appreciate the arts and crafts as much as the psychic and spiritual talents. Some of the crafts taught in this school are leather working, blacksmithing, jewelry, pottery, horse handling, hound mastery, building, culinary arts, and many other professions similar to those of humans. All of the handmade products of these crafts are intricately decorated with designs and Fay writing.

For those learning the skill of blacksmithing, the craft goes far beyond what humans usually expect. The Fay learn how to set precious stones in metal, forge swords and make armor, as well as construct anything needed to be formed out of metal. However, the metal workers do not use iron of any kind, as the touch of iron is poisonous to both the Fay and the elves. To prevent poisoning from armor, swords, and other products, these are all made of a type of metal unknown to humans. The armor is padded inside with soft wool and leather, and the sword hilts are tightly wrapped with thick strips of leather or made of magickal woods. The weapons, armor, saddles, and garments are highly decorated with magickal Fay designs and words, as well as beautiful symbols and nature scenes.

Some old stories of faery activity mention wars, in which one band or group fought another, for reasons known only to them. These battles may be over territory, kidnapped royalty, or a queen, if the warriors are the Small Folk. Or the wars may be ones between the Seelie and the Unseelie Courts. The Seelie Court, Unseelie Court, and the elves are all known to have very gifted warriors.

The other School of Learning is much more advanced and very specific in the teaching, because it emphasizes the mental, emotional, and spiritual talents that are needed for guidance and survival of the Fay community as a whole. The specialty of warrior also teaches the greatest in physical coordination and battle skills with many types of weapons.

Training in eight of the first ten levels is needed to become a special Healer-Monitor. These Fay monitors, male or female, oversee each group of the Small Folk and are specially trained for this purpose. The Fay understand that the Small Folk are a subspecies closely akin to them and have taken on this responsibility because the smaller faeries can be so capricious, frivolous, and unaware of danger to themselves. The Healer-Monitors watch over the little groups of Small Folk, advising and teaching them whenever they can, trying to keep them out of trouble as much as possible. If the danger level becomes too great, the Healer-Monitors have the authority to call in the Fay warriors.

Bards

The Fay bards learn to play several musical instruments, including the harp, fiddle, drums, flute, bagpipes, and other wind instruments. Not every bard qualifies for voice lessons. It is the responsibility of the bards to entertain and instruct the community and all faeries through music. They travel often, showing up even at the smallest communities or near the solitary faeries. By singing and playing ancient songs, they teach and remind all faeries, young and old, of their cultural heritage and history. Bards are required to learn the same Fay and human histories as the historians.

There are eleven specific classes of study in the more advanced school: bards, companions, councilors, foretellers, guardians, healers, historians, magicians, mystics, teachers, and warriors.

They also use their talents to help the magicians create magickal energy to heal nature and help the warriors in battle and the healers in their work. The academic and master bards are capable of changing negative vibrations into positive ones in any situation.

Male or female, Fay bards usually travel alone or pairs. At times, Fay bards have taught their music and songs, such as the legendary "Londonderry Air," and skills, such as the MacCrimmon clan's extraordinary ability with bagpipes, to certain humans. Not all of their music is the soft, melodic tunes we expect; it covers all kinds of rhythms known to humans.

Since the Unseelie Court has the same types of schooling, there have been times when bards of the Seelie Court and Unseelie Court competed against each other for control of a situation or person, or fought with music to turn vibrations positive or negative.

The bards also surreptitiously keep an eye out for possible trouble when traveling and report any such incidents to their king and queen. No human ever travels through Faery Land without it being known.

Companions

Fay companions are carefully chosen, for their studies and responsibilities encompass compassion and discernment of intent. They work with faeries, many astral beings, and humans in an attempt to instill hope in difficult situations, comfort in sad times, and encouragement to start new projects or lives. They also project a sense of friendship and spirituality when needed. Sometimes they form a personal attachment to specific humans, especially those who become quite close to the realm of the Fay and Small Folk.

Councilors

This group is taught diplomacy, rules, and justice. They work closely with the council of elders. They are a kind of judge and jury, settling private, family, or community disputes. It is their duty to advise the king and queen on all matters that involve more than one clan of Fay or the Small Folk. They are also involved in any disputes with other magickal beings or humans. Councilors are taught to present all possible sides of a problem with every possible solution.

When necessary, they pass sentences on offenders of the Faery Laws. The most severe sentences include permanent banishment from the clan or community or imprisonment within rocky mountain prisons where the offender is kept in a semipermanent state of sleep for several years. During this sleep, the offenders' subconscious minds are continually bombarded with the reenactment of their negative deeds, until they either die from the experience or become truly repentant. This is a punishment reserved for extreme offenders. At the end of this time, the offender is either accepted back into the Fay community, banished to the Unseelie Court, or required to turn to a solitary existence as if they did not exist.

Foretellers

Dreams, visions, and omens are held in high esteem among the Fay. The foretellers use all the prophesying methods known to humans, as well as the ancient Secret Faery Oracle explained in chapter 14. Foretellers are taught how to accurately interpret all these methods, as well as how to use all kinds of divination tools to help petitioners who ask for their help. Like the bards, they may wander about their world and this world as well. They work closely with Fay healers, magicians, and mystics. They are frequently teachers of humans who are seeking to learn a particular type of divination or how to interpret dreams. Foretellers frequently live in towers where they have a clear view of the heavens, for they also study astrology and astronomy.

Guardians

The Fay who study on this level are prepared to guard certain sacred places in Faery Land and on the physical plane. On the earthly plane, they dwell in large groves of trees and the high mountains, and along coastlines, as well as in unexpected power spots. Humans might consider them a type of magickal forest ranger. They pass on messages to the Fay magicians and healers when any of the Small Folk tell them of diseased flora or animals. When the situation is hopeless, they contact the Fay mystics, who perform rituals of passing or dying.

Healers

Fay healers specialize in treating all aspects of the Fay or elf, including the physical, mental, emotional, and spiritual. They also work at healing psychic diseases and wounds. They work with crystals, stones, herbs, and the elements, as well as physical methods, such as pouring in energy with touch. At times, and for their own purposes, they may intervene and heal humans. Shamanism and meditation are still the preferred Fay methods of communication with humans who seek help or knowledge.

Historians

The historians work especially hard to accurately record and remember all the history of Faery Land, the human world, the ancient gods and goddesses, and all of the shamanic realms from the beginning of Fay time. Fay history started long before human history did. Their historians work with the Fay councilors in advising possible actions on certain events by reciting what has and hasn't worked in the past with similar events.

Magicians

This group of students studies all the effects of the elements and astral and universal energies upon all the worlds and their inhabitants. They learn how to weave these energies into magickal spells. Their studies also include ancient astrology. Basically, they are the teachers of magick for the Fay, the Small Folk, and humans, in understanding positive and negative energies, how to use these to better a life or for protection, and how to travel through each of the levels of Otherworld safely. They often teach humans during sleep. On occasion, a magician will become a human guardian or guide. Members of the other classes can become guardians, guides, or lovers as well.

Mystics

The members of this small group of Fay spend much of their time working in spiritual realms far higher than either the physical or astral worlds. In a way, they are like high priestesses and priests, as they guide their people in a spiritual, religious manner, and plan and lead all such ceremonies. They preside at coming-of-age rituals, bindings (marriages), deaths, and the crowning of a new king or queen. They also lead all the seasonal celebrations. It is their responsibility to advise the king and queen when the court should make its seasonal moves to a new place.

Teachers

These students are involved with individual groups of the Small Folk, such as those Small Folk who care for flowers, trees, and such. It is their responsibility to teach the Small Folk what they need to know in order to fulfill their duties. They work closely with the Healer-Monitors of each little faery group. Some of these teachers also make certain that the young Fay learn to read and write in the ancient faery script, and learn Fay history before they go on to one of the two higher Schools of Learning. The teachers often recommend certain younger Fay to the masters and elders for further intense training.

Some of the older Fay teachers teach those humans they consider worthy. They might use riddles and verse as a way to weed out those who do not have the dedication and true, deep desire to master the ancient techniques and knowledge. Many of their methods of teaching are reminiscent of Zen teaching. Others use more direct forms of teaching and answer questions. Often these teachers will not allow themselves to be seen but appear behind the student during meditation; the student hears only a distinct voice and may feel the touch of a hand on the shoulder or head.

Warriors

Although the majority of this group are male, there are some Fay women who are admirably suited as warriors. They are called upon during times of peril. The warrior class trains with all types of weapons and in all kinds of conditions. They even learn a weaponless method of fighting that is similar to the Oriental ways on Earth. It is the responsibility of the warriors to protect the communities and inhabitants from vicious wild animals or rogue Fay and elves, such as certain exiled members of the Seelie and Unseelie Courts. They also must protect against any astral creatures and the occasional unfriendly human who manages to wander into their realm. If they befriend a human, they can become a guardian of that person. Fay warriors can be found in any astral or earthly war or struggle of positive energy against negative energy. Since the Fay do not make positive or negative judgments, except in the purest forms, their help or refusal to help is rarely understood by humans.

Some of the Schools of Learning have very few students at one time, with the candidates being carefully screened; only the very best are admitted. In other categories—such as teachers, healers, warriors, and a few others—they have as many students as can qualify.

The Fay community in general is as complex as that of humans, if not more so. Each Fay has individual characteristics, as do humans, but as a culture their insight on, and reaction to, various matters and behaviors can be very different. If you are approached by a Fay from either court, you should be cautious and very polite until you learn what that particular Fay is like as an individual.

Do not assume that a Fay from the Unseelie Court is evil or bad. The Fay from this court are simply another cultural group, with different ways of doing things and beliefs in certain ideas. Often a Fay from the Unseelie Court can give you help and a perspective on a problem that would not come from a Seelie Court member.

Meditation to the Fay

Begin your meditation with the relaxation techniques described in chapter 2. As with all meditations in this book, you can read the following meditation into a tape recorder so you can fully relax and follow along with it.

You are standing at the edge of a forest of tall trees. A dirt pathway winds through the trees until it disappears from sight in the dim sunlight that filters through the thick branches. You hear the faint sound of a flute and begin to make your way down the path into the forest. You hear the call of birds all around you.

In a short time, you reach a fern-filled glen with a small stream running through it. It is very sunny as you stand at the edge of the glen and look across at another forest, just like the one you just went through. Suddenly everything is quiet. The birds are silent; the soft lilt of the flute has stopped. You hear the sound of footsteps behind you. You turn quickly and find yourself facing a tall Fay. He is dressed in a tunic and trousers in shades of green. He has a bow slung over his shoulder and a long sword at his side. His long black hair is tied at the back of his neck with a strip of leather. His slightly tilted green eyes watch you closely, as if he can see straight into your mind and thoughts.

"What do you seek in this forest?" the Fay finally asks.

You tell him that you want to meet the Fay and learn from them.

"I am a warrior and prince of this clan," he says. "Come with me, and I will show you safely through our kingdom."

The tall Fay leads you across the stream on a series of stepping stones. Within minutes, he takes you through a short section of the next forest. Before you are tall cliffs with Fay houses and the Schools of Learning built of crystal and natural materials right up the sides of the cliffs. Under the edges of the trees surrounding this palace of the king and queen and their courtiers stand more rustic, but still elaborate houses where many of the Fay live.

He takes you into the palace to meet his parents, the king and queen. They talk to you for several minutes about the importance of bringing the knowledge of the existence of Fay and Small Folk back into the human world. The king emphasizes the need for caution when sharing this information, lest you bring harm to yourself.

The prince then takes you to one of the schools, where you talk to a few of the teachers. You stop at the kennels where the hound masters are letting very young faery pups play in the sunshine. Their white coats shine in the sun; their ears and eyes contrast as blood red.

From there, the Fay takes you to a meditation cave inside the cliffs. The inside of this cave is completely lined with all colors of natural crystals. There are padded benches against the walls. Lanterns hang in four locations, signifying the four directions and the four elements. Between two lanterns, half in the shadows, sit a man and a woman, both dressed in white robes with colored insignia embroidered on one shoulder.

"Elders," the Prince says, bowing in front of them, "this is a human traveler in Faery Land. This human is a believer in the Fay and the Small Folk and is here to learn more about us."

"This is permissible," answers the male Fay. "You may ask us two questions that have importance in your life."

You ask the questions and listen carefully to the answers, which may be in riddles or prophetic language instead of being straightforward. The faeries rarely give a straight answer to a human, as they like to make us think about and reason out the answer.

"We must go now," the prince says. He motions toward the cave entrance.

You walk ahead of him, and as you step outside, you find yourself back in your physical body.

Now is a good time to write down the answers you received from the elders so you can think about them.

Dance and Chant to the Fay

To attract the attention of the Fay and to express your interest in being friends with them, you can dance under the light of the full moon and chant:

> Oh, Keepers of the knowledge old,
> Come Fay, so tall and bold.
> Build a friendship here with me.
> As I wish, so may it be.

Leave a single flower or leaf in the center of your dancing area as an offering of friendship.

Calling a Fay Guardian

Asking for a Fay guardian is a great responsibility. You cannot choose which Fay you want but must take the one sent to you. Guardians are chosen to best balance the positive traits you lack in this life. If you reject their teaching or turn away from the advice of the Fay guardian, the doors to Faery Land will be forever closed to you. You may still see the Small Folk as they go about their daily living and playing, but you will no longer be able to communicate with them. You will not ever see the Fay again.

Begin by sitting quietly, thinking about what improvements you need to make in your physical, mental, and spiritual lives. When you feel ready, go for a walk in nature. Choose a calm, quiet place where there are few if any people to interrupt you.

When you feel drawn to a tree along your path, sit down with your back against the tree. Listen with your heart, and soon you will sense the sap moving about inside the tree. Your senses will move out around you until you sense the life in every single plant near you. Whisper this chant:

Seladone, Seladone. Greetings to the wise Fay.
Masters and teachers of the kingdom of the Fay, I beg of you a boon.
Send to me a Fay guardian who will teach me many things.
One who will warn me of harmful things and help me improve my life.
Seladone, Seladone. Hear my plea, O mighty Fay.

Stand and walk back down the path toward home. As you go, you may feel a presence behind one shoulder. The farther you walk, the stronger the presence becomes.

This is your Fay guardian. Any name the guardian reveals will not be his or her true name, as the Fay strongly believe in the power of personal names and so they guard them. Greet your guardian each morning and ask for aid and guidance often. This way, you will build a strong connection with your guardian.

Asking for Faery Gifts

Faery gifts are either tangible objects or psychic talents, such as the second sight. Often, the faeries will put a black or pure white stone in your path so you will find it. This special gift is filled with faery power to help you in your studies of faery knowledge and also for personal protection from negative members of the Faery Realm. If you find such a stone, show gratitude by saying:

I thank you for this stone of power,
And send you blessings in this hour.

If you wish a psychic talent to evolve, you need to determine which one interests you most and to take action on your own. This takes the form of investing your time, energy, and efforts in the talent and reading what books you can find on the subject. These talents may be reading tarot cards or runes, healing, automatic writing, predicting the future, psychometry, using a pendulum, or working with crystals and other stones.

You want to attract the very best faery teacher possible, and this will be one of the Fay. Wait until a full moon for this ritual. On a small, flat altar, inside or outdoors, arrange objects that represent the four main elements and spirit. Place a small bowl of water or a seashell in the west; several lit candles for fire in the south; incense for the perfume carried by air in the east; and a small vase of wildflowers, a mossy stone, or a bowl of fresh soil for earth in the north. Spirit is in the center. There, you might want to place a small figure of a faery or some other object that reminds you of spirit. The faery statue is symbolic of your friendship with the Faery Folk that is leading you into new pathways of spiritual growth.

Stand or kneel before your altar and say:

Mighty Fay, both wise and old,
Your teachers are unsurpassed.
I ask you to send a teacher bold
Who will work with me upon this task,
Of awakening talents deep.
Let my mind with knowledge burn.
Let answers come while I'm asleep.
And teach me until I finally learn

What is needful to help humans, Folk, and Fay
As I walk the difficult faery way.

Place the fingertips of both hands on the edge of the altar, so that your Fay teacher can build a bond between you. Bow briefly before the altar because you can be certain the king and queen are present for this powerful ritual.

In the days to come, you will find yourself led to people and books who express the beliefs in the talent your Fay teacher wishes you to know.

Chapter 5

The Small Folk

The Small Folk—the little, winged faeries—are related to the Fay. However, they are easier to contact and work with, especially if you are doing something in nature. They, too, will aid you in gaining knowledge and desires. Since the Small Folk live under the guidance of one of the specially trained Fay, they can directly present your requests to their more intelligent, powerful guardian.

The Small Folk tend to live in many little groups, divided according to their work and interests, as well as the cultural area in which they live. Each little group of the Small Folk has a king and queen. In addition to tending to their special duties in nature, the Small Folk love to indulge in feasts, dancing, music, and general fun. They can also be very mischievous and troublesome if you annoy them.

Most of the Small Folk have wings like those of little butterflies. The wings are also collections of massed energy that enable faeries to move

As with the Fay, the Small Folk species includes both good and bad individuals. Since these smaller faeries prefer laughter, fun, and happiness in all its forms, they will ostracize disorderly faeries, forcing them to live solitary lives until they change their ways. If these recalcitrant faeries continue to cause trouble, they are not allowed back into the clan.

quickly from place to place. The few who do not have actual wings still have the ability to project massed energy for movement from between their shoulders.

Like the larger Fay, the Small Folk can be guardians and guides to human beings. This is the truth behind the tales of the faery god-mothers. In reality, there are faery godfathers too. The Small Folk have always been friendlier to humans than the larger Fay, perhaps because throughout history humans felt less threatened by a creature much smaller than themselves and so did not fear them as much as they feared the Fay.

Although all faeries live by the premise that life should be lived in balance with nature, they also firmly believe in spirituality and com-munion with the God and the Goddess. However, the laws of the Small Folk tend to be more frivolous and quite often less mature than those of the larger Fay (more on these later).

The Small Folk love to ride on hunts, although they do not kill animals. Their festivals and celebrations are frequent and elaborate, always accompanied by dancing and music. They are more apt to engage in mini-battles between clans than do the Fay. And they are usually more friendly toward humans, although they can also be trick-sters and mischief-makers on occasion. They have a propensity for bor-rowing books and other human-owned objects without asking, and returning them at strange times, such as when you think you will never find that object again. Have you ever known exactly where a book was on a shelf, removed those books all off the shelf, and never found the one you wanted, only to have it returned to its place at a later date? That is faery borrowing.

Asian folklore is full of tales of faeries, most as old as the cultures themselves. Faeries are considered very powerful, able to take on outra-geous disguises to fool humans. Some, however, prefer to keep a human-like appearance. One of the Asian Small Folk is the Chinese House

Faery. These little beings make their rounds of a neighborhood at night, checking human houses and families to see which ones they want to live with. They do not like messy housekeepers, and look closely at the pots and pans, because that is where they like to rest. The Chinese House Faery seems to have one mission in life: to help the housekeeper keep an even cleaner dwelling. Since today's Chinese House Faeries are found around the world, you may, unknowingly, be hosting such beings.

The Chinese Small Folk's castles are built between high mountain peaks and reached by a road of shining jade and silver. The buildings glisten with gold and colorful agate. The castles are frequently hidden by mists and clouds, or made visible only to those who take the time to look for them.

In Chinese faery lore, the Small Folk have a royal faery palace on the moon, known as Kuang-han kung, or the Palace of the Boundless Cold. When the full moon rises, look carefully at the lunar shadows and you may catch a glimpse of this marvelous place.

The Japanese believe that trees, rocks, water, and mountains all have their special faeries. However, the easiest Japanese faery to attract is the *kobito,* which is about the size of an ant. They live in small holes in the ground, usually near human houses because they have a great liking for human food.

Another small Japanese faery, the *tengu,* lives in the woodlands, particularly in the regions that are rarely entered by humans. These tiny beings have bird beaks and shining wings that flash in the sunlight, and they often carry fans. Able to disguise themselves as any animal, the *tengu* are guardians of the woodlands.

The only time you may meet the Japanese Snow Queen is on a crisp winter night. She brings snow and paints frost on the windows as she silently walks through the moonlight. She has night-black hair and eyes, and her skin is as white as snow. She rarely speaks and has little to do with humans.

The Small Folk of Korea are the strangest of all Asian faeries. They are a little larger than those of Japan and can disguise themselves as slugs and snails. In this manner, they creep about the plants they tend.

England is full of faeries, both the Fay and the Small Folk; however, the Small Folk predominate. Those of the woodlands love to dance in the moonlight. Frequently, their circle dance turns a ring of grass a darker green or causes a circle of tiny toadstools to appear at the edges of their dancing ground. If you find one of these places, you will know it is a faery ballroom. To make friends with these faeries, leave a tiny cup of milk with a little honey or bread with butter in the center of the ring for them.

May has always traditionally been faery month. Actually, this time period includes the entire month of May and part of June, ending with the summer solstice. Every moonlit May and June night, the Small Folk have lavish parties, congregating in their most splendid clothing. However, don't bother looking in the woods for these festivals, for you won't find one; they are held underwater and can be seen only when the light of the full moon shines upon the water's surface. Then you may see the spires and towers of faery castles deep under the water.

The ancient land of Ireland is also full of faery stories. There, the Small Folk prefer to live under grassy hillocks with cleverly hidden doors. It is considered dangerous to be around these hills at night, for the Small Folk sometimes kidnap humans and keep them in Faery Land. However, if you are brave enough to put your ear to the ground of one of these hills, you may well hear the faint sounds of faery music and revelers inside. At least one famous Irish harpist dared to sleep on a faery mound—and awoke with an entire medley of new songs in his mind.

One way to make friends with Irish Small Folk is to leave treats on their hillock-homes. Give them such things as strawberries and cream, ribbons, butter, or polished stones. The Small Folk will not actually take the physical object. Instead, they cut away its shadow, or essence, and take that with them back to Faery Land.

Irish Small Folk, like all other faeries, are often invisible. However, there are certain ways to know if one of the Small Folk of any culture is near. If a flower bends slightly, one of them is either on it or working around it. If an entire section of flowers bend at the same time, it is possible that a faery king or queen is passing by. A sudden gust of wind frequently marks the passing of a royal faery procession either traveling from one place to another or simply surveying their kingdom.

The Small Folk are more frivolous than the larger Fay. However, they take great pride in their work with nature and the elements. They know that praise is a universal, cosmic song that emanates from everything and everyone on Earth. Without it, nothing would exist. So the Small Folk sing songs of growth and love and celebration to all the plants and nature objects in their care. Most human adults have buried their desire to praise and have forgotten its importance. Each of us needs to rediscover this ability to praise everything, so all things and people will grow in the designed cosmic manner. This will also help us to grow and expand our consciousness.

Working with the Small Folk presents you with many positive possibilities to benefit you personally, your immediate area, and all of nature. For these are the works

If you catch a glimpse of the elusive Irish leprechaun, do not take your eyes off him for a second or he will disappear. As long as you watch him — and especially if you are holding a four-leaf clover — he can't disappear. However, it is useless to try to get him to reveal his hidden treasure of gold, for he is full of tricks and deceptions that will keep you from getting it. It is best to make friends with him, for his presence around your home will bring good luck.

the Small Folk concentrate on. They accomplish this through music, singing, and dancing with joy. To them, every moment of every day is a reason to celebrate and praise the Goddess and the God for their lives, their work, nature, and the universe. Befriending the smaller faeries may also attract their own wise men and women, who can discern the truth in your heart and soul. If you pass their criteria for goodness, these little wise ones will share with you ancient nature wisdom that has been long forgotten on Earth. You will find yourself feeling more at one with all plants, learning to hear their individual songs of being, and understanding their purpose in life. You will also be taught how to communicate with nature in its entirety—a great gift for celebrating all life.

The Small Folk live everywhere on Earth, even in places you would not expect to find them. Their forms and appearances differ depending upon their location and what work they are doing. The faeries of the gardens will not look like those who tend desert plants, for example. The Small Folk live a rather carefree life in comparison to the Fay, for they rarely build any permanent structures, although they will use any manmade small structure that is available, such as an empty birdhouse or a garden toad house.

The best times to see and communicate with the Small Folk are called the faery hours: dawn, noon, dusk, and midnight. Midnight is the usual time for their celebrations, music, and dancing.

Has some object or book that you wanted suddenly disappeared, only to reappear at a later date? The Small

True faery dust is not the twinkly glitter that is shown in movies; it is the act of a faery, either Fay or Small Folk, sharing their breath with a human. Faery breath contains tiny particles of inspiration that make a human feel so inspired in their creative areas that they feel like they could fly.

Folk have borrowed it. Sometimes this borrowing is a trick to make you recognize their existence, sometimes it's simply fun to them. Other times, they seem to want to use the object or read the book. (Remember, all the faeries, both the Fay and the Small Folk, know every language spoken on Earth, including those we now consider extinct.)

Since the Universal Rhythm permeates everything, the faeries respond to this power by dancing to it. When they appear to be flying, they are really moving their bodies around atoms and molecules very quickly to get from one place to another. They link themselves to the universal rhythm while dancing to it. This is easy for them, as faeries have an internal awareness of sound and rhythm at all times. They understand that, even though it may not appear so, everything moves to an internal rhythm.

If you desire to "fly" in your career, artistic hobbies, or with a friend or life mate, you must get in touch with your internal rhythm. This includes your passion for life, your own special sounds and colors. Then you will understand how to dance around the rhythm of everyone else and "fly" to your goal.

Again, the Small Folk's laws tend to be less serious than those of the Fay—more like guidelines and explanations of natural rules than laws. However, the faeries take their laws very seriously. The laws describe an action or quality that is found in both Faery Land and in

"Flight of fantasy" is a good phrase to describe the act of a faery sharing its breath with a human. This sharing is rarely done because during the transference the faery actually shares the essence of who she or he is. Therefore, faeries are very careful to choose only very special humans to do this with, as sharing forms a bond with that particular human. All they ask in return is your acceptance of their existence and presence in the world.

earthly nature. Among the faery laws are spirituality and communion with the God and the Goddess in nature. By learning to work within these simple laws, you can change the very fabric of your life.

The Law of Power states that every living thing has within its nature the willingness to grow, to change, or to stretch to new heights and depths. This is real power. When something stops growing, its power is lost. However, the faeries understand that nothing has an end, not even growth. It may end its cycle in that form, but the ending is the beginning of another cycle in another form. Thus, everything is interconnected. When human adults accept the idea of this connection with everything else on Earth and in the universe, they reveal their own individual true power.

This idea also applies to what humans term "time." Since everything is interconnected and there are no true endings, Faery Land has an atmosphere of timelessness. Time is a human-conceived idea and has nothing to do with reality.

The Law of Compassion has little to do with love and much more to do with tolerance. It is wrong to try to love everyone and everything, because it is impossible. This only ends up making you feel guilty when you can't. However, you can think of yourself as a giant garden that includes the person or thing or idea as if it were a natural part of the garden. You don't have to love it, but you can acknowledge that they are part of the life cycle. You can use the same technique with qualities about yourself with which you are uncomfortable.

The Law of Beauty has nothing to do with physical beauty, for that kind of beauty is in the eye of each human beholder. This law applies to the beauty of surrender. Everything in nature, even faeries and humans, is in a constant state of surrender, or vulnerability in its purest form. We have no choice, for this is a natural occurrence that no one can avoid. Faeries are the bravest beings who frequent this planet. They remain where they are regardless of what happens, for they are responsible for certain areas of nature. They surrender to whatever happens to them or to the plants within their area. They stand still in the face of every great natural event, knowing that whatever happens, it will bring beauty and incredible change with it.

Choose one experience or quality in your own life that you have trouble accepting. Embrace this quality and acknowledge its right to exist. Gradually, you will learn to stand still instead of running and hiding from things that upset you. As you stand still and accept, you will find those experiences losing their power over you, or the quality changing into something more acceptable.

Gardeners who love what they do add to the life-spirit, making the plant faeries stronger. Humans who simply enjoy looking at gardens and nature add to the faeries' pleasure also.

The garden immediately feels it when an individual faery or a group of them steps outside the dance of pleasure, which is what keeps plants alive. Faeries will withdraw if too much pesticide is used, for they are very sensitive to such things. They will also stop their celebration dance if there is ill will or unnecessary violence among the nearby humans. Their withdrawal causes the plants droop. In rare cases in which the problem is not resolved, the faeries have the ability to hold back the rain.

> The Small Folk have this all-encompassing principle in their lives: Always take time to do what really pleases you, in body, mind, and spirit. A faery's pleasure is not the same thing as what humans consider pleasure. It is a constant celebrating of the life-spirit within a garden or within all of nature. It is this life-spirit that keeps a garden alive.

If the gardener is to blame, all the immediate faeries will send loving intent to correct the situation. If that doesn't work, they may resort to mischief of all kinds, large and small. If necessary, they may even buzz around the gardener like an invisible swarm of bees, singing so loudly the gardener may hear them. When the gardener stops to listen, the faeries send joyous, loving feelings to the human, subtly changing negative emotions into positive ones.

The creation of true pleasure begins with your heart, body, and emotions rather than your mind. So you need to begin to pay attention to your relationship with your physical body and emotions. Take note of small things that truly please you and brighten your day. Do you feel guilty if you feel pleased and happy? If so, you must choose one thing a day that is pleasing to you and do it. Sitting beside a plant, strolling in a garden, or walking in a nature setting will help add to your pleasure and teach you to accept the existence of pleasure in small ways and in everything.

As with pleasure, magick is in everything. You need to train yourself to look deeper and in a wider scope to begin to see this magick. And be certain to celebrate what you find by acknowledging its existence and importance in the cycle of all things. The power of magick comes from a much higher plane of the universe and is available to all who understand how to tap into this power. This power is neither positive nor negative; it merely is.

The Faery word for fear is *wronged-love*. They rarely experience it with other faeries, but it can arise with humans. When uncaring humans change the land for development, the faeries of every plant and tree within that area begin to fear. No one has acknowledged their domain or existence. They become extremely upset, thus affecting the vibrations of the entire area around them. The early Native Americans knew how to handle this. They always asked permission before cutting a tree or killing an animal; they also left a peace gift of tobacco or corn. If humans would acknowledge the existence of the faeries in the area they plan to change by leaving a small gift of friendship, land developers or people making large changes to their yards would have fewer problems and find that fewer things go wrong.

If you want to find true love and a mate, the faeries advise you to begin by praising yourself, by revering your life with all its strengths and struggles. Praise everyone and everything around you. Be genuine, though, and fill your life with beauty. This will attract a true love into your life.

Faeries are filled with magick and special powers. However, they also have needs—needs that help them to evolve and grow. If a faery falls in love with the human she or he is teaching to love a plant or tree, the faery learns the feeling of passion. Passion is actually a growth spurt that breaks through to a higher state of evolution for faeries. Faeries to whom this has happened can then inspire humans to their greatest creative ventures. If you are fortunate enough to be touched by faery passion, there are few restrictions to what you can accomplish. However, you may have to make decisions and changes in your life, and that makes most humans uncomfortable.

To the faeries, the process of creating a new life, or sexual pleasure for joy, is called singing. They recommend that you make love only with someone for whom you feel deeply. Otherwise, your creative powers are wasted. Making love can create more than a child if both partners focus on the same goal. This is part of the mystery behind the tantric practices of India.

Among the Faery laws are spirituality and communion with the God and the Goddess in nature.

Although faeries do not live forever, the Small Folk can live for up to five hundred years, while the Fay may live to be one thousand years old. When faeries complete the mission for which they were born, they "marry the earth," which means they merge with the physical elements. If you are open to Faery Land, you may hear the song of the merged faery at the spot where she or he joined the earth.

Through the centuries humans have sighted numerous faery funerals. The mourners accompanying the coffin show true grief. No one has ever found a faery grave, so this may be another way of "marrying the earth," one that is reserved for royalty and entails more elaborate preparations than for ordinary faeries.

To the faeries, enlightenment doesn't involve moving higher up but moving to the earth, or deepening. This is a slow but majestic process, one that brings with it extraordinary magick that can change your life forever. When you reach the highest state, you feel as if nature has completely wrapped its arms around you. Your senses are opened to such an extent that you see and know things you would have missed or never understood before. Truths are revealed that may be surprising to you.

Faeries sometimes encounter blockages in their paths just as humans do. However, instead of becoming upset, the faeries dance and sing to the blockage, accepting its existence. By praising its right to exist, they can easily move through it.

Adult humans can use much the same method when encountering physical, mental, creative, or emotional blockages. Recognize the blockage's right to exist; praise and celebrate its being in your life. If you find yourself full of anger about the blockage, dance sharp dances and "sing" in a journal. Sharp dances are moves that are jerky, not flowing, for example, a sword dance. "Singing" in a journal is writing out your feelings in prose or poetry. Soon you will be able to walk through the blockage to the path that lies on the other side.

Although meditation and astral travel are ways to reach Faery Land and make contact with faeries, the contact is easier and more natural if you can do it out in nature. Open-eyed faery sightings are rare, even for those gifted with faery sight. The best way is to relax and watch around you with half-open eyes. Doing so helps you make a shift in consciousness that make faeries more visible. Faeries are extremely sensitive, and they cannot be ordered to appear. Instead, invite them to join you in meditation, contemplation, or ritual. They love the scent of jasmine, so burn jasmine incense to entice them to join you. Or, drink jasmine tea.

You must always be honest with the faeries. Never gossip about them; if you do, they will either shun you or become a constant nuisance during everyday life, meditation, and ritual. And never try to capture a faery; they will make you pay for that cruelty. If you deliberately desecrate a faery spot or sacred place, or if you show disrespect for the planet and nature, the faeries may place a curse on you that could last for generations.

The harmful faeries and their kin are most active during the last quarter of the waning moon. If this type of faery enters your house, you can expel it by burning a white candle anointed with cinnamon, clove, or bay oil; ringing a bell loudly; or sprinkling salt in the corners of each room of the house. You may also carry burning incense throughout the house, particularly frankincense, myrrh, sandalwood, cinnamon, or clove. Then ask that the house be filled with only positive energy.

If you work spells and rituals with faery help, it is best to repeat the spell five times. And never ask the Small Folk to come into your protective circle, for they easily get bored and like to play tricks and tease. If the Fay appear inside your circle, it is because they want to, not because you asked.

You can learn much about nature and plants from the Small Folk. Even though they are more mischievous and frivolous than the larger Fay, they have an important role to play in nature. Appreciate them for themselves and the duties they cheerfully undertake.

On occasion you may meet a solitary faery, living in a wild part of the forest or an overgrown meadow. They are very shy and do not trust humans. If you are still and patient, you may be able to catch a glimpse of this strange little being, dressed in leaves, moss, and patches of cast-off animal fur. It is highly unlikely that you will ever be able to make friends with the solitary faeries. Simply acknowledge their existence and appreciate their uniqueness.

Small Folk Chant

The first thing you want to do when moving to a new place or learning about the Faery Folk is to issue an invitation to all the Small Folk to be guests in your home and garden. Since they are cautious, it may take them time to gather in groups great enough for you to notice the effects of their presence.

Plan to do this welcome chant inside your home at dusk or midnight. Have three white candles burning in holders in the room where you will do the chant. Sprinkle a little ground ginger or put a fresh slice of ginger root onto a saucer and set this out as an offering. You may need a small compass if you are unsure of true earthly directions. You will also need a small chime and a striker.

Face the north. Strike the chime once and say:

> From the land of exotic snow crystals,
> From the dark green of forests and the whitest of snow,
> I bid all faeries welcome here.

Face the east. Strike the chime twice and say:

> From the golden lands of sand and desert,
> From the palaces of the djinn, and the milkweed faery of China,
> I bid all faeries welcome here.

Face the south. Strike the chime three times and say:

> From the islands in the great oceans,
> From the tropical forests and flowers,
> I bid all faeries welcome here.

Face the west. Strike the chime four times and say:

> From the lands of mountains high and forests deep,
> From hidden lakes and secret sacred places,
> I bid all faeries welcome here.

Now, if you wish, you can use a very ancient seer's method to see any faeries in the immediate vicinity. The first time you do this you will be distracted by the strange position in which you must stand. However, you may see blurred movement in the room.

Stand on your left leg and hold your right leg up off the floor. Hold your right arm straight out from your body, with your left arm at your side. Squint with your left eye while keeping your right eye closed. (This sounds very simple until you try to hold yourself still in this position for more than five seconds.) At the same time, scan the room for signs of the Small Folk.

Although this chant calls and invites the Small Folk, you will find the Fay are not far behind in taking up residence. They are far more difficult to see, appearing only as shadows.

Spell to Recover Borrowed Objects

The Small Folk are notorious for borrowing various items from humans and sometimes forgetting to return them. Sometimes this is done because the faeries want to enjoy the object for a while; other times, they take something to guard it for you.

The Small Folk always borrow my books, small items off my desk, and pieces of jewelry. However, when confronted, they readily admit they have the object in question and return it in a few days. Only once did they not admit they had the object I sought, nor did they return it for some time. I suspect this is because the Fay, not the Small Folk, "borrowed" the item.

We had listed our house for sale. It is not pleasant to sell a house you have grown to love, and it's even worse to have people you don't know tramping everywhere during open house. Beside my wedding rings, I had only one other ring of value: a small emerald ring given to me by my husband for our anniversary. After one of the open houses we hosted, I decided to wear the emerald to dinner. When I opened the drawer, its familiar place was empty! We looked through every drawer in the small chest, thinking I had not put it back in the same spot. However, we never found it.

I was heartbroken but put that emotion aside during the chaos of moving and caring for a very sick spouse. After a month or two, when life resumed a more or less normal pattern again, I opened the jewelry drawer to put away earrings. There, in its customary place, sat the emerald ring.

My husband grinned. "The faeries took it so that woman wouldn't steal it." Being psychic, he continued to describe one of the open-house visitors who had made me uneasy. "When she looked in the jewelry chest, the one ring she would have stolen was gone."

When I tried to thank the Small Folk, they assured me it had not been them. That left only the Fay, and they were not making appearances at that time. The Fay rarely involve themselves in such petty deeds, so this event was extra special.

So, if you fall victim to a faery borrowing, you may have to bargain to get the item back or wait until they tire of it, at which time they will return the borrowed item to the exact place you knew it to be in before it disappeared. If the "borrowers" do not return the item, and you need it quickly, you can perform the following ritual, which offers an item of exchange.

If you do it outdoors, place your exchange offering in a sheltered area, the flowerbeds, or even the nearby forest. If done inside, place the offering on your altar. Suitable exchange offerings are small polished stones or crystals, a beautiful flower in summer or holly with berries in winter, or a few drops of wine in a tiny cup. Even a necklace made of strung acorns or pinecone petals is acceptable. Then say the following:

> *Hobbity hawdaw, hippity kline.*
> This gift is yours; the taken is mine.
> If you did not take, the truth make known.
> The culprit's name will then be shown.

Rap three times on the ground or altar as a symbol of opening the door between Faery Land and this world, then say:

> I open the door without a key
> That a free exchange of property
> May make us strong friends as all can see.
> This is my wish. So shall it be.

Although the offering gift itself will not disappear, the faeries take its essential power and its shadow. After three days, put or pour the gift outside on the ground. Soon you'll find the borrowed item right where it should be.

Protection Against Mischievous Spirits

Sometimes, no matter how careful you are or how friendly you are with the faeries, you will find your home invaded by malicious, unfriendly faeries and the negative spirits that hang around with them. You will know they are present because children will have nightmares, a feeling of uneasiness will invade one or more rooms, or a sudden streak of bad luck will occur.

There is no point in nicely asking these troublemakers to leave—they won't. You must take the attitude that they do not have a right to be in your space, and you are going to force them to leave. You will need salt, red thread, a tiny piece of amber with a hole through it, and a short piece each of oak, ash (rowan), and thorn (hawthorn or blackthorn).

Start by calling the Small Folk to your aid while you pour a small amount of salt into the palm of one hand. Say, "Faery Queen so bright and good, bless this salt with the highest of positive powers."

Then chant:

> King and queen of Faery Land,
> Relieve me of this troublesome band.
> I also call the warrior Fay,
> To send the evil ones on their way.

Moving clockwise around each room, sprinkle a few grains of salt into every corner, including closets. Repeat this in every room until you have blessed the entire house.

Gather the pieces of oak, ash, and thorn together in a bundle. Wrap the red thread around the wood until it is firmly bound. Before tying off the thread, slide the tiny bit of amber onto the thread and finish the tying. While binding this bundle, say:

> Oak and ash, lammer (amber) and thorn,
> Red thread binds the evil born
> Of faeries bad that sow sour seed,
> Removes all evil at great speed.

Place this bundle in an inconspicuous 'spot' or 'area' in the open, not in a drawer. Consider placing it behind a photo or on a bookshelf.

Whenever your house feels completely safe and clean again, in about a month, bury the magickal bundle so the power it has gathered is returned to the earth.

Request for a New Love

Faeries, especially the Small Folk, are always sympathetic to lovers or those looking for a lover. If you want their help in attracting the right person for a love, begin by giving them an offering of a little honey in a small amount of milk. Set this either on your personal altar or outside in a sheltered place where the Small Folk can feast without disturbance.

Take a tiny splinter of fir and one of poplar. Put the splinters of wood into a mortar and pestle, along with three hairs from your head and three dried rose petals. Grind these together until they are well mixed. It is very difficult to grind wood into a powder, so just do the best you can. Put this mixture into a jar or a small plastic bag.

Preform this ritual at a crossroads, a faery circle, or your garden. A breezy day is best, but any day will do if you feel you must do the spell. To be most effective, perform the spell at dawn, dusk, or midnight.

Pour the mixture into your hand and say:

> Small Folk of power,
> Help me in this hour.

Now, with the mixture on the flat palms of your hands, begin to turn in a circle, chanting:

> True love of mine, come to me.
> This is my wish. Now shall it be.

Turn faster and faster as the mixture blows off your hands and sifts away between your fingers. When it is all gone, bow to the Small Folk and say:

> I thank you for your grace and aid.
> I know this spell is solid made.

Go home without looking back.

Chapter 6

Faeries of Earth

The Earth Faeries are responsible for working with the substance from which everything is made and from which everything comes. As was mentioned earlier, this substance is universal energy. Therefore, these particular faeries are adept at handling and directing universal energy into the areas of the earth where it is most needed. They are particularly active after natural or human-made disasters.

This type of faery is also the most adept at shape-shifting, as she or he must move about freely when at work without attracting attention. Sometimes they work alone, other times in a group, depending upon the needs of any given area. You may see a beetle, bird, frog, or some other animal common to that region and never realize it is a faery—unless you have trained yourself to see faeries and look beyond their disguises.

Each Earth Faery carries two small crystals that come from other planets in the galaxy. One is dark colored, the other clear. They use the dark crystal to draw out all negative energies caused by the disaster. Then they use the clear crystals to direct the universal energy into the earth to heal its wounds. They

Earth Faeries are so busy they rarely take the time to befriend humans. You can gain a measure of friendship with them by working to restore a damaged area, such as by planting trees and sowing native grass and wildflower seeds.

are always joined by the local faeries whose plant charges have been damaged or destroyed. Instead of "marrying the earth," the local faeries who have lost their plants may choose to become responsible for new, similar plants that sprout. This is why life frequently returns quickly to damaged areas.

If you are very fortunate, one of them may show you how to direct universal energy into the earth, a technique you can use to heal people as well.

Earth Faeries use their special crystals for this work. However, humans can accomplish much the same thing, but on a smaller scale, by holding their dominant hand palm up to receive the universal energy, and their other hand, palm down, toward where they want the energy to go. Humans handle only small amounts of this powerful universal energy, whereas the Earth Faeries withstand and direct a thousand times more than humans can.

To honor these faeries and gain their goodwill, recite the following chant:

> Good and bad we all must see,
> A cycle through eternity.
> Teach me to help remove Earth's pain
> And make the planet whole again.

Offering Stone for Good Luck

Throughout many countries, one can find sacred stones. These may be in gardens, along paths, or placed in odd places in the landscape. If you look closely, you will see that libations of some kind have been poured over these stones for centuries. In the Celtic countries, the libation is milk mixed with honey. In the Mediterranean, it has always been wine. In Oriental cultures it was often rice wine or honey.

To help your faeries celebrate the eight holy days, place an offering stone in your garden for good luck. The stone may be of any fist-size shape, or it can be a flat piece of rock. Place it in among your flowers, not quite out of sight, yet not quite hidden.

Take a small amount of libation (in this case wine) in a fancy glass. As you slowly pour the wine over the stone, softly chant:

> Belief and friendship I offer you.
> All faeries of this planet, I answer true.
> May you fill my life with joy, peace, and love,
> Good luck, good health, and blessings from above.

Faery Ointment or Oil

Through the centuries, there have been hundreds of recipes for faery ointment, usually compounded to help one see faeries. With the right ingredients, this is entirely possible. However, mistranslations were often made and poisonous ingredients were added to some of the recipes.

Other uses for faery ointment are not as well known.

- A drop of the ointment can be put on the center of the forehead of a sick person to help pull out the illness.
- A drop of ointment can be placed on the threshold to repel negativity.
- A drop of ointment can be placed at each of the four corners of your property to ward off intruders and signal to faeries that this is safe ground.
- A drop of ointment on the sole of each shoe before an interview or meeting with an attorney can do good. The uses are endless.

You will need either a number of small bottles, ideally dark colored (clear bottles must be stored in a dark place), and labels to mark what is in each bottle. You will need as much morning dew as you can collect in five days, as well as at least two cups of cold-pressed almond oil, three four-leaf clovers, a three-inch sprig of thyme (preferably flowering), and the petals of one fresh red rose, one fresh white rose, yarrow flowers, and marigolds.

Clean a tall, wide-mouthed, lidded jar with scalding hot water. This will decrease the possibility of mold.

Put the oil into the mixing jar. Break the herbs and flowers into small pieces and add them to the oil. Set the filled jar in a safe place where it will get sunshine for most of the day. Leave it there for seven days. Each day, mash down and mix the herbs and flowers in the oil with a wooden spoon. Always carefully recap the jar to keep out contaminants.

When you first add the ingredients to the oil, and on each of the seven days when you stir the mixture, softly say:

> Faeries of the night and day,
> Faeries of the moon and sun,
> Guide my efforts in this task
> Until this magick spell be done.

At the end of seven days, bring the jar inside and prepare to strain out the plant material. To do this, you can use several layers of cheesecloth secured with clothespins to the rim of a very large glass measuring cup. Or, you can use a cone-shaped coffee filter lined with a paper filter. The latter method will strain out more plant residue than the first.

Squeeze as much oil as possible out of the cheesecloth or filter. Put the remaining plant residue on a barren spot so it can be blessed with life.

Clean the small bottles with scalding hot water. Fill them with the faery ointment and label each one. When all the bottles are filled and labeled, hold your hands over them and repeat this chant three times:

Healers of the mighty Fay,
Bless this ointment here today.

Store in a dark place until needed.

Chapter 7

Faeries of Air

The Faeries of Air represent the breath that gives form to every word and thought. This means not only the physical act of breathing in and out but also the spiritual breath that is needed to manifest desires or create

events. It behooves you to be careful what you dwell on in your mind, or what you often speak about, for you will manifest it at some time, depending upon the depth of the emotions you attach to the thoughts. You become what you think and speak, so try to think and speak in a positive manner only.

Since these faeries work constantly with air, they can influence winds and storms. They love to ride the strong currents of windstorms. You can call upon them for help to calm the storm, if you appeal to their sense of responsibility to the earth.

Air Faeries are difficult to see, as they are almost as transparent as

This type of faery sometimes shows humans that they are obsessed with the wrong desires. In this case, stop and give serious thought to what you want in your life. Go over every detail of the event or person involved, then take the time to gather more information. If an Air Faery has warned you about your desire, invariably you will discover some strong negative information that will, ideally, make you change your mind and your goal.

wind. If they are nearby, usually you will only see a faint outline or feel a tiny breeze brush against you.

To make friends with Air Faeries, use this chant:

> Light and subtle, helpful and fair,
> I greet these faeries of the air.
> Please help me to reach my goal
> Of balancing body, mind, and soul.

Be aware of how much your thoughts and words are negative or positive in the course of one day. If you find the negative dominating, make a conscious effort to change.

Chapter 8

Faeries of Water

Water Faeries are responsible for the Water of Life—the inexhaustible source from which every living thing gets its nourishment—all living things on Earth require moisture or water to survive. These special faeries work diligently with the water creatures and the Small Folk responsible for the plants growing around any body of water, large or small. They try to keep the life-giving fluid as clean and nourishing as possible. This frequently puts them at odds with humans, as we have a bad habit of being careless about pollution of earth, air, and water. On occasion, you will also find these faeries around garden fountains, large or small. Their affinity with water enables them to control the weather to a certain degree, especially rain, which adds to the nourishment of the earth.

To draw the attention of Water Faeries, recite the following chant:

Water Faeries represent the emotional and spiritual worlds of both faeries and humans. They can help control emotions or gain ground in spiritual development. However, one must work hard to gain their trust and cooperation. It is best if a human has already befriended the Small Folk and the Fay before attempting to contact and work with the Water Faeries.

Water of Life, the streams and the sea,
All of these are important to me.
I promise to help as much as I can
To reduce all the damages done by man.

Be certain you use water wisely and do not waste it. And keep your fountains clean and clear of debris. Water Faeries notice and appreciate humans who know the value of the Water of Life.

Seashore Spell

Sometimes humans need to thoroughly cleanse their auras, minds, and spirits. Negative things happen and keep happening until they feel as if they are so weighted, they will never be able to get up and keep going. Water has always been known for cleansing and healing and for work with the emotions. One of the strongest cleansing places is the shore of an ocean. (The second strongest place is a high, thundering waterfall, especially one that flows into a lake. These areas are full of Water Faeries.)

Bring a stone or flower to the seashore as an offering. One thing is always repaid with another.

Sit beside the water for some time and truthfully consider everything in your life that makes you feel suffocated, chained, and useless. Walk to the water's edge as a wave, or the tide, is beginning to come in. Write a word for each problem in the sand with a small stick. When finished, take a step back and softly chant:

Faeries of water, the oceans and sea,
I call upon you to purify me.
Wash out the ill and disperse the dread.
Fill me with calmness and hope instead.

Show me faery beauty, a new path to walk,
Beside me you go, as you cleanse with your talk.
My spirit lifts high. My heart is set free.
For strong love is sent between thee and me.
Lay your offering next to the words in the sand.
I bring you a gift to rebuild your power.

Bow politely to the unseen faeries who are hiding among the rocks and coves. Then walk away, knowing that the incoming tide will wash away your troubles, and the faeries will bring you guidance and knowledge so you can better yourself.

Ritual for Rain

The Small Folk are serious at times, but they much prefer to be jolly and merry, enjoying every minute of life, even when there is such a thing as a troublesome drought. Offer a little ground ginger for their cooperation, then prepare to act more childlike than grown-up. Dance in a circle around the offering, or, with your arms out, spin round and round like a top. While you dance, chant:

Rain, fall down on hills and town,
Water fall on one and all.
Rain clouds gather and change this weather.
What's dry, make wet. Great moisture get
To dampen flowers. Bring on the showers!

Keep chanting and dancing until you can do no more. Lie down on the ground, face to the sky, with your eyes closed. Visualize great black clouds pouring out fat drops of rain, then sheets of rain so thick you can't see through them. When you have done all you can, go about your business, knowing your chant will be fulfilled.

Chapter 9

Faeries of Fire

Of all the faeries, the Fire Faeries are the least friendly toward humans, possibly because their responsibilities are so great. They represent the creative energy that consumes and transforms everything it touches. Nothing in the universe is static; everything is always changing, however quickly or slowly. Even as the wood consumed in a fire transforms into particles of smoke, heat, and air, so the particles of everything that is consumed become something else. Nothing ever disappears; it only changes form.

Some of the Fay fall into the Fire Faery category, depending upon their spiritual strength and experiences. They have reached this point in their lives by being wounded through mental pain for what is happening on Earth. However, they still maintain a

Faeries of Fire also represent the intellectual and conflicting world in which we live. We are coaxed into believing that greater intellects among humans will solve the world's problems. The world is conflicted because it is out of balance: too many intellects with little or no belief in faeries, too few creative people. This does not mean that we should not acquire all the knowledge we can. But with this comes the responsibility to keep our balance with the faeries and the earth, in addition to using common sense.

melancholy joy and great strength with which they bravely battle the darkness in the world.

The forms of Fire Faeries waver constantly, as does an actual flame. They wear clothing in shades of red, orange, and yellow, so they resemble flames—if you are lucky enough to see one. Do not invite Fire Faeries into your home. This is far too dangerous, as they always carry the universal form of fire with them. If you leave a candle burning in a room with the lights off, you may catch a glimpse of one dancing in the candle's flame. The Fire Faery is dancing and praising the existence of the fire and everything it represents.

Use the following chant only to praise the Fire Faeries and ask their help in mental inspiration.

> Oh, Faeries of Fire, so bright and clear,
> I praise your presence of inspiration here.
> Fill my mind with possibilities great
> So that creativeness creates my fate.

Dispelling Anger

Fire Faeries are dangerous when their help is not properly and respectfully asked for. They quickly take offense, so don't order or speak sharply to them. Fire Faeries are excellent at helping dispel inner anger, but this is a spell you can do only for yourself. You can't hope to dispel another person's anger. It is best done on a new moon.

You will need a red candle in a fireproof holder set to the back of your altar, a metal bowl or cauldron in front of the candle, a four-by-four piece of white paper, and a pen or pencil. Write "I FREELY GIVE YOU ALL MY ANGER" on the paper and fold it in half. Lay it on your altar beside the cauldron.

Light the red candle and say:

> Faeries of Fire, Faeries of Light,
> I humbly ask your help this night.
> I want to control my anger inside
> That calmness and peace may abide.
> I give to you a symbol of that trait to burn,
> And know you will help me to make the return
> To the faery path that teaches power and dignity.
> If this is your will, then so it shall be.

Light the folded paper from the red candle. When it is burning well, drop it into the cauldron and say:

> I freely release this negative power,
> To rein it in better, beginning this hour.

Let the candle burn for twenty minutes before extinguishing it. As part of your personal improvement, meditate for twenty minutes each day for as long as you feel it takes to control your anger. In the meditation, see yourself in a very peaceful scene, beside a lake or in a deep forest meadow. This will release your tenseness and fill you with serenity and peace.

Small Folk Spell for Prosperity

To the Small Folk, prosperity means pots of gold, valuable jewelry, precious stones, anything shiny and showy. In the human realm, it sometimes means the same things, however, it can also take the form of a new love, a new job, an opportunity for good health, protection from the cold, food on the table, and clothes to wear. Prosperity has many facets. Faery power will give you the kind of prosperity the faeries know you need at that moment, so it is best not to ask for a specific thing—unless, of course, you have talked it over with the Small Folk and they are in complete agreement.

Prosperity needs the universal fire of creation in order to manifest. So, although the Fire Faeries are the trickiest with which to work, they are also important to include in your faery communications. Without universal fire of creation, there is no manifestation and therefore no prosperity.

Purchase or make a very small talisman bag. To make one, cut out two three-inch squares of cloth. Sew the squares together on three sides, leaving one side open. You will also need one small package each of silver and gold seed beads, a little piece of pyrite stone, a tumbled piece of carnelian, and a cotton ball scented with bayberry or honey-suckle oil.

Take a large pinch each of silver and gold seed beads and add them to the bag. Say: "Although prosperity starts small, it is shiny and bright."

Put in the pyrite and carnelian stones. Say: "The glitter of gold is symbolic, as the orange speeds the manifestation of this spell."

Add the scented cotton ball. Say: "As with burning incense, oils give the sweet smell of success."

Sew the open end of the talisman bag firmly closed while chanting "Each stitch I sew will make this spell grow."

You can now carry the bag in your pocket, pin it to the inside of your jacket or blouse, or place it under your pillow at night.

As thanks to the Fire Faeries, burn a candle for twenty minutes for five consecutive nights.

Chapter 10

Faeries of Plants and Forests

Most humans who become faery friends are most familiar with the faeries of plants and forest. They are more numerous than the other types of faeries, easier to befriend, and more likely to let you see them.

These faeries like beautiful, exotic, brightly colored clothing. For a hat, they may wear a foxglove blossom. Or they may carry a pansy as an umbrella. They love to curl up on a petal of their plant or flower and sing praises to it. Sometimes they fall asleep, and you may be able to see one. Being full of energy and mischief, the younger faeries like to swing on floating cobwebs or ride on dandelion fluff or bubbles.

If your plants are well cared for, these faeries will help you all they can. If you deliberately neglect your plants, you may start having little problems about the house. This is the faeries' way of punishing you. They can become a considerable nuisance with their tricks and mischief. The only way to placate them is to start caring for your plants and, as a peace offering, leave out bread with butter and a little honey on it.

The Plant Faeries live the closest to humans because of flower gardens and wildflowers and grasses growing along the sides of roads. This type of faery includes those that care for the shrubs humans grow in their yards and the potted plants they put on their porches or decks or inside the house itself.

Plant Faeries also love to celebrate. They are constantly dancing and singing, even at night. Oftentimes their orchestra is the sound of crickets in the grass. They feast on flower nectar and little cakes made of pollen. If there are berries in the vicinity, they include those in their celebration meals.

The Forest Faeries are more aloof than the Plant Faeries. Only hikers into deep, undisturbed areas are likely to catch a fleeting glimpse of a Forest Faery. These faeries are very shy and wary of strangers in their domain. They understand the human need to clear wind-blown trees and even to cut the trees themselves. As long as reforestation is practiced, the Forest Faeries make no trouble. They understand the cycle of growth and ending. What they do not understand are humans who damage their trees by driving spikes deep into the trunks or cutting deep markings through the bark into the wood. This is wanton destruction in their minds, just as not replanting would be.

You need to let both types of faeries know that you appreciate their efforts in making the world more beautiful. Cooperate with them as much as possible, and your garden and shrubs will flourish.

Contacting Solitary Fairies for Nature Wisdom

The solitary faeries gain much nature wisdom, for they take the time to observe nature constantly. Some of them have left the Schools of Learning to be alone for meditation and self-introspection, and to gain firsthand knowledge from living in and with nature on a daily basis.

Although solitary faeries are found in ordinary and extraordinary places, the very wise ones live in the wild places—the deep forests and high meadows, the jungles and untraveled rivers, the bare peaks along a hiking trail, or the marshes filled with cattails, moss, and grasses.

Solitary faeries often wear long robes or loose trousers and tunics, the colors of which blend in perfectly with their surroundings. They are slow, thoughtful speakers with long silences between answers. They have learned to communicate with every living creature in their area, and they can read the elements. Seeking out a solitary faery for wisdom is best undertaken only by those who have learned patience and the skill of listening carefully to every nuance of sound around them. To be chosen as their student is a great honor.

Chapter 11

Faeries of the Deserts

Of all the faeries, these are probably the most exotic looking. The areas where they live vary from pure desert to semidesert. However, their forms are basically the same wherever they are in the world. They are so transparent that you can see completely through their bodies. The only way you know it is a faery is that the spot where it lingers or flies is wavering constantly. You might mistake the rough edge of the faery's wings for the legs of such desert insects as grasshoppers, cicadas, or locusts. Most of these faeries do not bother with clothing, as they consider it too fragile and confining when working the spined plants that frequently grow in these areas.

There is no plant whose size is too small or whose life span is too short to warrant the attention of the Desert Faeries. They sing constantly to their plants; their songs of praise and growth are soft but can be heard on the winds and among the animal sounds at night.

If you decide to grow desert plants, such as cacti, in your yard or inside your home, you will discover that these exotic faeries will have a

Desert Faeries tend to any plant that grows in semi- or full desert conditions, even if the life span of that plant is very short, growing and flowering only during the short rainy season. They also care for the plants in the oases and around the water holes of the deserts, whether large or small.

presence as long as these plants are healthy and thriving. You will have an up-close chance to befriend the Desert Faeries and perhaps learn desert magick from them. They know all the secrets of the deserts.

Their songs of praise differ greatly from those sung by Flower Faeries or Forest Faeries, for example. These songs sound more like gentle desert breezes, with the words getting softer, then louder, then soft again.

To gain their friendship, you might try the following chant:

> Desert Faeries, old as time,
> Hear my friendship in this rhyme.
> Soft as desert breezes blow,
> Bring me knowledge I need to know.

It will take much patience on your part to befriend these faeries, for you must learn to listen very carefully to the slightest of sounds to hear them.

Three Wishes

Although the djinn (or genies, as they are called in Western cultures) originated in sandy, rocky, barren areas of the Middle East, today they live in places all around the world. They are a very mobile species of faery that enjoys travel. According to their species' rules, if a human sees them, they must grant three wishes.

The best way to attract the djinn is to lay out a display of Middle Eastern jewelry, cloth, or clothing. Put a gold-colored candle near, but at a safe distance from the display. Place an offering of a small amount of yogurt on a plate. Also, have ready three small, decorated bottles with corks or caps. Make certain the bottles are of different colors or shapes, so you can remember which wish is in which bottle.

As you sit and wait patiently for the candle to flicker in a sudden dance, think seriously about the three most important wishes you would want in your life. When the golden candle begins its dance, say the following:

O djinn of the deserts, the winds, and the sands,
Arabic faeries who travel the world for mental delight,
The most powerful faeries of many lands,
Fill my bottles with three desired wishes this night.

Point to the first bottle. Clearly state your wish. Wait a few moments before corking or capping the bottle. Repeat these steps for the remaining two bottles, then say:

I thank you, O djinn, for helping me.
As with your will and mine, so shall it be.

Extinguish the candle. Put the bottles of wishes in a safe place, where you will see them every day. When a wish is fulfilled, remove the cork or cap of that bottle so the faeries may cleanse it to be used again.

Chapter 12

House Faeries

House Faeries are the friendliest of all to humans. It is very common for one or more of them to attach themselves to a particular family or person. Oftentimes, the family attachment will continue for generations. Other times, faeries will attach themselves to a particular house. These are always the Small Folk, not the Fay.

Among those faeries who attach themselves to a family is the Irish leprechaun. Leprechauns will follow a family from house to house for generations. That is why they are found around the world, in every country where Irish immigrants settled. The same action is found among the brownies and several others of the faery kin. Other Small Folk who prefer to live with humans also have developed this trait, probably because of the mobility of society these days.

House faeries keep the sick company, quietly sing to cranky babies, play with pets, and try very hard to keep the atmosphere of the house positive so humans feel relaxed, comfortable, and safe every time they enter the dwelling.

The presence of House Faeries is a very fortunate circumstance, and you should treat them with great respect. They take a great interest in the prosperity and well-being of the family and will help in any way they can to make desires and wishes come true.

They have also been known to warn humans of any danger that may threaten them or the house.

The only problem one might have with a House Faery is that they love all living creatures, including mice. Sometimes it becomes necessary to specifically state to your House Faeries that you do not allow mice to live in your home, and that, if necessary, you will set traps to remove them. The House Faeries will then try to discourage the mice from entering the dwelling.

House Faeries are quite small but very energetic for their size. They love cleanliness and order. So if you find papers rearranged on your desk, crumbs brushed off your table, or small clean spots on your large kitchen floor, you will know your House Faeries are doing their best to help you.

Because of their fondness to the person or family, House Faeries make good liaisons between you and other faeries. For example, if you are having difficulty getting a particular houseplant to grow, they will seek advice on your behalf from Plant Faeries. If you aren't meant to have that plant in your home, they will sadly tell you that it will die, and they will guide you to another kind of plant that will flourish and improve your home atmosphere.

If the vibrations inside your house become less than desirable, your House Faeries will enlist other faeries talented in removal of negatives to help you cleanse the atmosphere. Since House Faeries communicate with all species of faeries and are friends with dragons and other magickal beasts, do not be surprised if you find yourself playing host to Chinese House Faeries or gargoyles, for example. In fact, if this is the case, consider yourself very fortunate—your House Faeries are getting the best beings to protect, nourish, and better you. That means they have accepted you as part of their unique family.

House Faeries are rarely taller than three to four inches. They dress in old cultural styles, usually related to whatever cultures your family came from. Here is a generalized description of a European House Faery: The females wear their long hair rolled into a bun atop their heads, wear a long dress with an apron and soft slipperlike shoes, and carry a broom. The males generally wear knee pants with suspenders and a white shirt, long stockings to the knees, and soft leather shoes or boots. They also carry a tiny sheathed dagger at their belt. It is very difficult to tell the age of a House Faery, for they all look middle-aged.

House Faeries love to sing as they work. Usually their voices are so light that a human has difficulty hearing them. At the full moon, they have feasts and rituals, but they always see that everything is left clean when they are finished. At the solstice and equinox, they may leave your home for a few days and travel to the gathering place of other faeries to celebrate with them. Often they will leave a guardian creature behind until their return.

As with all of the Small Folk, you are more likely to see a flash of light or movement from the corner of your eye than to see them completely with your physical eyes.

House Faeries, like other faeries, do not like lazy people. You must do your part in housekeeping and rituals. Never lie to a House Faery; if you do, they will leave you immediately. In fact, do not lie to any faery! You will end up with more trouble than you care to think about.

Appreciate your House Faeries, for you are truly blessed to have them with you. Show your appreciation by leaving them a small cookie or piece of cake and a little glass of juice after a ritual or at least on the full moon. You want to remain on friendly terms with this class of faery so they will continue to live with you and bless your life and home.

If you don't know whether you have House Faeries, you can perform a small ritual to ask them to make themselves known to you or to call House Faeries from elsewhere into your home.

House Faery Ritual

First, clean your house or apartment as thoroughly as you can, including the windows. House Faeries appreciate clean windows so they can watch what goes on in the neighborhood.

Place the following items on a table where they will not be disturbed for several hours: a white candle in a fireproof holder, a small bowl of water, a tiny glass of juice, and a cookie on a plate. If you wish, you can light a stick or cone of floral incense, placing it in a proper incense holder. House Faeries love the smell of flowers. If you do not want to burn incense, at least put a small bouquet of flowers in a vase and add that to your ritual items.

Light the candle. Stand before your arrangement of items and raise both hands as if welcoming a good friend—which you are—and say this chant:

> Little faeries of the home, I greet and give you welcome.
> I ask that your presence lingers here, for I hold your friendship dear.
> In love these gifts I give, and ask that you with me live.
> Thank you.

Leave the candle burning for at least an hour. By this time, any House Faeries living with you or attracted to living with you will have taken the essence from the food and drink. Extinguish the candle. Pour out the juice and water. Throw away the cookie, as it will no longer contain valuable nutrition.

It will not be long before the House Faeries make themselves known in some physical manner. This may come as a flash of light or fast movement seen from the corner of your eye, or a pleasant odor that suddenly surrounds you in a specific area. You may have the feeling that something is messing with your hair. Or, it may be a fluttery sensation on your cheek. House Faeries are very affectionate with those whom they chose to live.

After you have invited House Faeries into your home, or greeted the ones who already live with you, you can strengthen the association by doing a meditation. This helps you become familiar with your own culture's House Faeries and their individual traits.

You can read this meditation into a tape recorder if you wish and play it back when you are ready to do the meditation.

House Faery Meditation

Choose a comfortable chair in an area where you are least likely to be disturbed by pets, the phone, or other people. If you want to mask background noise, you can play soft instrumental music.

Take several deep breaths and feel your body relax from your head to your toes. Visualize a brilliant white light surrounding you and entering your entire body with each breath. You can exit the meditation at any time you wish by simply thinking of your body. You will be fully protected and never in any danger.

Visualize an old-fashioned white picket fence with a gate surrounding a wild, overgrown flower garden and a quaint old house. Huge trees shade little tables and chairs throughout the garden.

You open the gate and walk up a path of stepping stones to the house. When you knock on the door, it is opened by a plump little lady in a long dress and an apron. She smiles up at you and invites you inside.

At the kitchen table sits a little man, just as plump, smoking a long-stemmed clay pipe. The pipe odor is not tobacco, but the scent of roses and lavender. Notice carefully what their clothing looks like, as this will give a clue to their cultural origins.

The faery woman brings a teapot to the table. "Sit down," she says. "We will share a pot of tea while we talk."

You see delicate flower teacups with wooden spoons beside them. A pitcher of milk and a bowl of nectar syrup mixed with honey are nearby. When the faery pours tea into your cup, you smell the delicious odor of jasmine. As she pours tea for her husband and herself, you glance around the room, noticing the different cultural decorations that adorn it, the quaint furniture, the embroidered wall hangings, the carved wooden cupboard filled with a variety of dishes, cups, and goblets. Braided rugs cover the floors; the little stove is enameled in white with flowers painted on it. Pots of herbs hang at the little windows. A little winged cat is sleeping on one of the windowsills.

"We have been waiting for you to visit us," the faery man finally says with a grin. "One should always know one's houseguests well."

"Please, ask us any questions you want." The faery woman smiles at you as she sips her tea. "We will answer any question we can."

(Pause for a minute or two on the tape for your conversation with the faeries.)

When you are finished, thank the House Faeries for their hospitality. Go back down the stepping-stone path and through the gate of the white picket fence.

When the gate closes behind you, you will find yourself back in your body, feeling refreshed and at ease. This is an excellent time for you to write down all you remember of the visit with your House Faeries.

You can repeat this meditation as often as you like. At times, the faeries will have you sit with them at one of the tables underneath the tall trees. They may even show you the rest of their little house or give you a tour of their wonderful flower garden.

As your friendship with your House Faeries grows, the atmosphere of your home will become more positive and inviting to other faeries. All who are interested in the Faery Lore should try to attract a good family of House Faeries to live permanently in their dwellings. These faeries keep the vibrations high, protect and warn the family and pets, evict negative faeries, and attract good fortune. House Faeries try to keep order when other faeries enter your home at certain times of the year. They are not always successful, as the host of a party cannot always keep the noise at a reasonable level. However, considering the value and friendship offered by families of House Faeries, you should try to attract such a family as soon as possible.

Ritual for Welcoming House Faeries

The first step is to thoroughly clean your house. All faeries dislike laziness and dirty housekeepers, and you will not attract a high quality House Faery if you have a messy home.

The second step is to sprinkle ground cinnamon, ginger, and cloves on a small baking sheet or glass pan. Heat this at a low temperature in a kitchen range, convection oven, or microwave until the spicy odor begins to work its way throughout the house.

It will not be long before you see tiny movements from the corner of your eye and feel wispy touches in your hair and on your face. Your House Faeries have arrived. Say the following:

Nikka, nakka, kolba, min,
You and I shall live as kin.

With this ancient rhyme you have invited the House Faeries to stay forever and to be your friends. Unless you insult them in some way, they are in your home to stay.

Each night, set out a clean bowl of fresh water on the counter. House Faeries are particularly clean faeries, and they like to bathe their children every night.

Spell for Brownies

Brownies are hard workers but very shy around humans. Still, they feel a deep need to live as close to humans as they can. It is very nice to have a brownie in residence. His purpose in the home is to keep tasks flowing smoothly and to maintain a peaceful atmosphere. When a brownie lives with you, work goes faster and easier, you seem to gain more satisfaction from what you do, and you have the peace that comes with knowing your household has another protector.

Oddly enough, if you praise them for their work or conspicuously honor them in any way, they will disappear and never return. And only one brownie lives in a house at any time.

If you feel you must praise your brownie, do it in a very careful manner. Saying: "Someone helped things go smoothly today. I certainly thank whoever it was, for it made my day happier."

Brownies are always lurking around, looking for a home to inhabit. I have had good luck attracting brownies by setting out gingerbread men or ginger cookies. (If you are fortunate enough to catch a glimpse of a brownie, the all-brown, hairy little creature will remind you of a gingerbread man.)

When you set out the cookies, say:

I wish that a brownie would listen and see
That I need a brownie to live here with me.

If you have a cat or a dog, it will see the brownie long before you do. The brownie will quickly become friends with your pet.

You, however, are on a different level, according to the brownie. The best thing you can do, even if you see him, is to ignore his presence.

Chapter 13

Faery Kith and Kin

Many beings and creatures move between the astral and physical worlds. Some of these are distant kin of the Fay and Small Folk or connected with them in some way. Some of them are not friendly and should be avoided whenever possible. Others are friendly and can be contacted for aid in certain rituals and problems.

The characteristics of these entities also show up in human personalities. If you are aware of the faery kith and kin, you can easily use your knowledge of them to sort out humans with similar personality traits—traits you may wish to avoid or to build on while cultivating a friendship or relationship of some kind.

At each solstice and equinox, great numbers of these entities gather to celebrate the harmony of nature and life itself. If one is very observant and aware, these are the

The same rules that apply to dealings with the Fay and Small Folk apply to working with the faery kith and kin. Treat them all with respect when you meet them—even those you deem mischievous and untrustworthy. Never betray their trust or try to deceive them. These negative actions eventually bring sorrow and very bad luck. To use the power of these beings in an attempt to control other people will turn the power back upon you.

best occasions to see faeries and their kin. At these times, the faeries often go on their Rades. Sometimes these Rades are an actual movement from one place to another until the next season; other times the procession is merely a company of Otherworld entities going to a celebration gathering spot.

In the following descriptions, the term "magickal uses" refers to a being's particular power on a special subject for spellwork or meditation. "Personality traits" means the traits of that particular being that you may also find in human personalities; by being aware of these, you can determine whether a relationship, friendship, or business venture is advisable.

Since people have immigrated from one culture or country to another for many years, it is now as common to see a Scottish brownie in China as it is to see a Russian *domovoi* in the United States.

Barbegazi

These gnomelike beings are native to the high mountains of France and Switzerland. They hibernate during the summer and are rarely seen when the temperature is above zero. It is difficult to tell the difference between the males and females. Their very large feet act as snowshoes or skis when they want to travel from one place to another, and are also quite useful for digging out of an avalanche or burying themselves in snow banks to avoid humans. Their long hair and beards look like icicles. They wear white garments that blend in with the snow, making them difficult to see. They communicate with each other by means of an animal-like whistle. To send long-distance messages, they make eerie hooting sounds; this is frequently mistaken for the wind or the call of an alpine horn.

The *barbegazi* build their homes near the summits of the highest peaks. There, they excavate an underground network of caves and tunnels, with many little openings to the outside world. These openings are disguised with hanging icicles.

These little beings are usually friendly toward humans, although they avoid them as much as possible. However, they have been known to warn local humans of approaching storms or impending avalanches.

Magickal Uses: Warning of and protection from storms and bad weather.

Personality Traits: Willingness to help others anonymously.

Bogies

Known as *boggans* on the Isle of Man, and *boggies, bog-a-boos,* and *bogles* in other places, this name refers to a wide variety of mischievous beings that prefer to live in partial or full darkness. Although they can be frightening, they are not usually harmful to humans. However, you should never invite these entities into your home or rituals, as they are extremely difficult to evict. If you find bogies in your home or office or living on your property, you should take immediate action to get rid of them.

These little mischief-makers are rather vague in appearance, if seen at all. Their wispy form is dominated by hollow, gleaming eyes. In Ireland, a branch of their species is known as the *ballybogs.* The Irish ones are very ugly and small, with long, thin legs and arms. Fortunately, bogies are not very intelligent.

Bogies will inhabit just about anything but delight in cellars, barns, hollow trees, abandoned mines, and caves. Indoors, they hide in deep cupboards and basements, under the sink, in cluttered closets, and in old abandoned buildings. Sometimes they infest school buildings, junk shops, tool sheds, secondhand stores, and law offices, where clutter is common.

They come out of their hiding places only at night when everything is quiet. Then they create such mischief as messing up stacks of paper or magazines, hiding articles you will soon need, spilling jars of jelly beans or other candies, mixing the colored clothes with the whites in the laundry, or pulling off the covers. One of their favorite tricks is to hover behind people until they make them very nervous. They also like to make muffled creaks and thumps that unsettle humans at night. Many of their characteristics are reminiscent of those of goblins and gremlins, although bogies fortunately are less imaginative in their tricks.

Magickal Uses: Avoid calling upon these creatures for any magickal aid.

Personality Traits: A person who enjoys making trouble for others.

Boggarts

This Scottish entity is a close cousin to the gremlin. In northern England it is called a *padfoot* or hobgoblin. Seen only as a hateful, solitary male, the *boggart* is short and extremely ugly; he is most active at night. He revels in tormenting and terrifying children.

Magickal Uses: Do not contact!

Personality Traits: A bully who enjoys threatening and harassing others.

Bokwus

This solitary creature made itself known to Native Americans of the Northwestern area of the United States. He is rarely seen, but his presence is felt in thick, dimly lit forests. The evil face of this being is always painted in bright war paint. Quick glimpses from behind tree trunks and the rustling of brush announce his presence to hunters, hikers, or fishermen. He is extremely dangerous to fishermen around rushing water of rivers and streams, because he waits for an unguarded moment, then pushes the fisherman into the water to drown.

Magickal Uses: Avoid using this being for any spellwork.

Personality Traits: A person who stalks or spies on others, meaning them harm.

Brownies

The original home of the Western European brownie is Scotland, although they have since immigrated to many other countries around the world, along with the Scottish people. Similar beings are known in North Africa as the *yumboes* and in China as *choa phum phi*.

The female brownies are rarely seen, so there is no recorded description of them. The male brownies are about three feet tall, with black eyes, slightly pointed ears, long agile fingers, and lots of hair on their bodies. Usually they wear brown suits, hats, and cloaks, which is how they got their name.

Brownies are friendly with humans and frequently will live in the house with them, bringing in good luck and happiness. Those who haven't established a home with humans reside in a hollow tree or abandoned building until they find the right family. They ordinarily are out and about at night. Cheerful and friendly, brownies naturally attract the attention and friendship of small children. They entertain the children, telling them stories or teaching them games. Although not fond of machinery, brownies will help adults with small tasks. Some brownies become so fond of a human family that they stay with them for generations.

The *bwbachod* ("boo-ba-chod") is a Welsh brownie that absolutely does not like ministers or those who don't take a drink now and then. The Manx cousin of the brownie is called the *fenoderee* ("fin-ord-er-ree") and looks very different from the Scottish brownie: ugly, large, and very hairy.

All brownies are offended by cheating, lying, messy people, and ministers. Their dislike of the clergy probably stems from the fact that ministers refuse to believe in the faery kin and call them minions of the devil. This statement is a contradiction in itself, for if one does not believe in something, then how could one classify it as evil?

Tradition says that you shouldn't ever give a brownie praise or a gift, or he will be insulted and leave. However, if the gift is small and given in secret and with tact, the brownie will not be offended. Like any other creature, they like to know they are appreciated. If you are fortunate enough to have brownies inhabiting your house, they will protect you against an invasion of goblins and other malicious beings.

Magickal Uses: Seek aid from these entities when you are in need of friendship, looking for a new home, or need to rid your present house of negative beings and energies.

Personality Traits: A person who enjoys working with their hands, as in gardening, crafts, woodworking, cooking, and such.

Chin-Chin Kobakama

These elderly but spry, elflike creatures live in Japan. The little men and women are active only during the day and like humans who keep up on their housekeeping. The *chin-chin* become a nuisance to messy housekeepers by making life miserable in a number of small ways. When they are content, they lavishly protect and bless the house and its occupants.

Magickal Uses: Help with finding a suitable house to rent or buy.

Personality Traits: A picky person who is only happy when things go their way.

Coblynaus

Their name is Welsh for "knockers." They are slightly different in appearance from those in Cornwall, being about a foot and a half tall and dressed like human miners. Although they throw stones at those who ignore or mock them, it is thought to be very lucky to hear the *coblynaus*.

The Germans know these beings as *Wichlein*; in southern France they are called the *gommes*.

Magickal Uses: Help with mining and prospecting.

Personality Traits: A person who mines or works with ores.

Cu Sith ("coo-shee")

This enormous dark green hound is said to roam the Scottish Highlands. It belongs to and is controlled by the Fay. It has a braided tail and human-size feet and only bays three times at night when hunting human women to become nursemaids for faery children.

Magickal Uses: Best to avoid this creature.

Personality Traits: A person who stalks the object of her or his desire.

Cwn Anwnn ("koon anoon")

This is the Welsh name given to the faery hounds. These animals are white with red ears and eyes. They are believed to be the hunting hounds of King Arawn of the Underworld, although in fact, each clan of Fay may have one or more packs of these faery hounds. These dogs became known as death-omen hounds, even though they do not cause destruction or hunt humans to death. The Celts generally called them "hounds of the wild hunt"; the Norse knew them as the companion-hounds of the goddess Hel and the god Odin. However, these white and red hounds appear in many tales of the Fay, sometimes as guides to Faery Land and other times as a barrier to those who are not ready to experience the magick of the faeries.

Magickal Uses: Finding guides to Faery Land and locating a faery companion. Seeking justice for misdeeds done to you.

Personality Traits: People who are employed as police, security guards, soldiers, or detectives. One who protects and guides others.

Domovoi

From the beginning of Russian and Slavic cultures, these small household spirits have lived with humans. The male, called a *domovoi*, is seldom seen, and the *domovikha*, the female, is *never* seen. If you should catch a glimpse of a *domovoi*, you might mistake his very small form, covered with silky hair, for a dog or cat. Seeing him is considered to be very bad luck.

Considered a benign being, the *domovoi* likes to live under the stove; his wife prefers the basement or under the house. If you move to a new house, put a piece of bread under the stove to entice the *domovoi* and his mate to move with you. It is thought to be extremely lucky for the family if a *domovoi* chooses to live in your house. If he mutters to himself at night, it is a sign of a pleasant life for the family. However, if he moans, misfortune is on the way. If he weeps loudly, someone in the family will soon die suddenly.

Magickal Uses: Good for calling upon to aid with predictions of all types, such as tarot cards and rune stones.

Personality Traits: One whose emotions and preferences revolve around the home. Emotions easily aroused.

Dragons

There are several different types of dragons. Their forms and sometimes their personalities vary from culture to culture. Most people are familiar with two of the types: Western and Oriental.

The Western dragon is the most leery of humans because it has been hunted for centuries and treated with disrespect. It has a heavy body; a narrow head on a long flexible neck; four legs; two long, strong wings; and a long, spiny tail.

The Oriental dragon is friendlier toward humans. It is respected in the East, and every year, on the Chinese New Year, long winding dragon forms are paraded in the streets and banners decorated with their images hang from house eaves. This dragon has a long, slender serpentine body, sometimes with legs, sometimes without. It is considered to be lucky and rules over all the elements.

Magickal Uses: Treat all dragons with great respect and never order them to do anything. If you become friends with the dragons, which are found everywhere, they will strengthen your magickal powers during rituals. Those that bond with you will also protect you and your loved ones, pets, and property.

Personality Traits: A person with a strong personality who carefully chooses friends and companions. One with leadership abilities.

Dwarves

Originally from the Scandinavian countries and Germany, these small beings now reside around the world. Dwarves prefer to live and work underground. They make their homes in great caves or tunnel systems, rarely coming to the surface except for certain celebrations. Northern Germans and Scandinavians refer to the underground dwarf homes as the Land of the Niebelungen.

Dwarves are about three feet tall, with large heads in proportion to their bodies. Their skin, hair, eyes, and beards are earth colors. Both the males and females have beards. Clothing types and colors vary from area to area.

Dwarves work closely with the vibrations of the earth, thus they have great power over rocks, stones, gems, and metals. They are also believed to be guardians of hidden treasures. Dwarves are recognized as the best blacksmiths and jewelers on this planet. Their work is doubly valuable because they imbue it with magickal powers.

They have a written language, which they use when engraving charms on objects or for sending rare messages from one group of dwarves to another. They also have an excellent oral tradition, with certain dwarves trained to remember their entire history both as a group and as a whole species.

Dwarves appear in many cultural histories, from Scandinavia to India. Their dress and appearance differ from area to area. In India, the Hindu god called Kubera fits the description of a dwarf. He is said to be small, with three legs and only eight teeth. He lives in the

Himalayas, guarding the treasures of the earth. Even though he is ugly, he wears much jewelry and travels from place to place in a magickal aerial chariot called Pushpaka.

German mythology tells of a small race of beings called the *duergar,* who live in the hills and rocks. They are experts in metallurgy; their specialty is the making of arms and armor, and they also work in gold, silver, iron, and all other metals. If you steal one of their creations, or gain it by coercion or force, bad luck will plague you the rest of your life.

Dwarves in Iceland wear red clothes; the ones in New Zealand wear long black robes. The ones living around Ebeltoft dress in gray jackets and pointed red caps and are said to have humped backs and long, crooked noses.

Although the Finnish people say that all dwarves are friendly if treated with respect, the people living on the Baltic Sea island of Rugen do not believe this.

On Rugen, they believe there are three types of dwarves: white, brown, and black. The white dwarves are beautiful and gentle. They spend the winter months inside their hill homes, making objects of gold and silver. During the summer, they come out at night to dance in the moonlight.

The brown dwarves are capable of making themselves any size they wish, although they are ordinarily only eighteen inches tall. They wear glass shoes and brown clothing with silver bells on their caps. These dwarves are very beautiful and have light-colored eyes. They are very fond of children and protect human children whenever they can. They also love to dance in the moonlight.

The black dwarves are malicious and very unfriendly toward humans. Ugly creatures, they wear black jackets and caps and keep very close to their hill homes. When they do venture into the human world, they do not dance or sing but sit in groups of twos and threes under elder trees. However, they are supreme experts in metallurgy, particularly in the working of steel.

Magickal Uses: Learning the powers of gems, stones, and metals, and how to use these powers in spellwork. Working for prosperity and financial security in your life.

Personality Traits: A person who loves jewelry or working with stones and metal. Can also be a person who prefers solitude and work to socializing.

Each Uisge ("ech-ooshkya")

This water-horse of the Scottish Highlands is the most dangerous of all faery water-horses. It roams around the sea and lochs and ordinarily takes up the shape of as a sleek horse that will let you ride it. (Other times it will appear as a handsome young man.) If a human mounts this water-horse, it will rush into the water, where it drowns and devours the victim. The Isle of Man has a similar creature known as the *glashtin*.

Magickal Uses: Very dangerous; not recommended.

Personality Traits: One who presents an attractive appearance but can easily destroy your reputation or career. A psychic vampire who drains off energy.

Elves

Elves and faeries are very close cousins, with many similarities in appearance, living style, laws, and behavior. Elves are of Scandinavian origin, and only became known in Britain with the invasion and settlement of the Vikings. In the Scandinavian language they are called *aelf* or *ylf* (masculine) and *aelfen* or *elfin* (feminine).

As a species, elves primarily are caretakers of the trees, groves, and forests of this planet. Most of them are benevolent and helpful to humans. However, some cultures, such as the German, treat them with caution, for elves have been known to have a bad temper on occasion.

Like the Fay, elves are human size or taller. They are quite beautiful, with slightly tilted eyes and pointed ears. Their hair color can be white-blonde, dark chestnut brown, or black; their eyes are vivid shades of green or woodland brown. Their skin shades range from pale ivory to a nut brown. Their hands are slender and graceful, with long tapered fingers. Elves have a very long lifespan, up to a thousand years, yet they can be injured or killed. Their aging only becomes apparent when they are close to the end of life.

Both Paracelsus and Socrates mentioned that the elves had crystal, alabaster, and marble palaces, as well as certain sacred places in nature. Because they have a king and a queen, and males and females are considered equal, elven society is obviously based on very ancient traditional ideas, perhaps a workable combination of humankind's matriarchal and patriarchal systems.

Like the faeries, elves have amassed great wisdom and ancient knowledge and can see into the future. However, they are not always solemn, for they have special celebrations and festivals. They dance, sing, and feast until dawn on these occasions. It is not wise for humans to seek out elves at these times, for they may be taken into Elfhame, just as the faeries sometimes carry off intruders.

According to Norse legends, there are two classifications of elves: light elves and dark or dusky elves. These categories are very similar to the Scottish Seelie and Unseelie Courts. Like the Unseelie Court, the dark elves will not deliberately harm humans. However, they are not on friendly terms with most humans either. If they wish to drive humans from their area, they will project negative energy to make humans uncomfortable or frightened.

Magickal Uses: Learning ancient knowledge and the skill of foretelling. Working with herbs and the arts.

Personality Traits: A person who seeks ancient knowledge so the world can relearn the old ways and make life better through changes.

Fox Spirits

These trickster beings are found in Japanese and Chinese lore. They are masters of illusion; if they want to steal anything, distance or security are no barrier. If you are a psychic, or trust your intuition, you can identify a Fox Spirit in disguise by the tiny point of flame above its head. To break the physical illusion, get the being to look into still water; the spell of illusion will be broken. If the Fox Spirit is over a thousand years old, the bark of a dog will have the same effect as the still water.

These unusual beings can live for thousands of years. If killed, they also reincarnate quickly. A very old Fox Spirit will have white or golden fur instead of the usual reddish color of foxes. Sometimes, it will even have nine tails instead of one. By the time the spirit reaches this age, however, it stops playing tricks on humans.

In Japan, the Fox Spirit is thought to be Inari, a goddess and the spirit of rice. A large temple dedicated to Inari stands in Kyoto and many smaller shrines to her exist around the country and in homes.

The Chinese believe these spirits cause misfortune and continuous accidents when they have been annoyed in some manner. People placate the Fox Spirit responsible by building a small house for it and putting out food and incense.

A type of Fox Spirit was known in ancient Lydia. When the Greek god Dionysus assumed the form of a fox, he was called Bassareus and was worshipped by his fox-skin-wearing priestesses, known as the Bassarids.

Magickal Uses: Beware of working with this being, as its ability to create illusions can fool you into thinking you have won your desire, when actually it will bring misfortune.

Personality Traits: One who is adept at playing mind games and can change personalities like a chameleon.

Gianes

These solitary wood elves of northern Italy dress in old-fashioned cloth-ing and pointed hats. They always carry a small spinning wheel in a back pocket and they use it to see into the future. They will not do spells for humans but will show humans how to do spells for themselves.

Magickal Uses: Foretelling, seeing into the future.

Personality Traits: A psychic or solitary practitioner.

Gnomes

These small creatures reach four to twelve inches high and take on the appearance of the people from the culture where they are found. They have been seen around the world, doing their weaving, woodworking, and healing, as well as caring for the plants and animals within their domain. They are closely tied to the earth.

In Germany, they are called *Erdmanleins*; in the Alpine areas of Germany they are known as *Heinzemannchens*. The Swedes named them the *nissen*; the Danes and Norwegians know them as the *nisse*. In differ-ent Balkan countries, they are called the *gnom*, the *djude*, or the *mano*.

Gnomes weave cloth out of animal hair, cast-off sheep's wool caught on bushes, and certain plants. They use this cloth to make their clothing. The female gnomes wear long skirts, blouses, aprons, and multicolored stockings with sturdy shoes. The males dress in similar stockings, red pointed caps, and long tunics. The older males wear a beard, and all married females wear a head-scarf. Since gnomes live for several hundred years, they do not marry young. Some of them have a large number of children.

Diligent workers, the gnomes harvest cereals and root crops. For certain occasions, they brew ale. They prefer to build their homes underground in the root systems of large trees in dim forests. However, these little creatures are very adaptable. You can also find them in rock gardens, thick shrubbery, and empty birdhouses. In addition to their main dwelling, which will have several exits, they always have other secret hiding places that they use for storage.

They prefer to work at their weaving, woodworking, healing, and aiding of the local plants and animals; they do not like human technology. Because of their strong connection with universal energy, which gnomes raise by dancing, they are valuable, magickal allies in the areas of influencing others for good and for healing. They also have the ability to see into the future. They are quite skilled at playing the fiddle and dancing.

Gnomes are rarely troublesome to humans. As benevolent beings, they are friendly to all creatures, including animals. However, if humans destroy their habitat, the gnomes have been known to cause great damage to equipment and to be responsible for mishaps that occur to the humans themselves.

Magickal Uses: Foretelling, music, dance, raising magickal energy for projects.

Personality Traits: A person who likes and aids animals. One who has close ties to the earth and the Old Gods.

Goblins

Although they are earth spirits, goblins are malicious and troublesome to have around. Tradition puts their origins in the Pyrenees Mountains. From there, they entered France, spread across Europe, and, by stowing away on Viking ships, made their way to Britain. They are called *Gobelins* in Germany and *brags* in Scotland.

There is a very slight relationship among goblins, brownies, gnomes, pixies, gremlins, leprechauns, elves, and faeries. However, other earth spirits will not allow goblins in their areas because of the trouble they cause with their malicious mischief and evil cunning.

Goblins usually look like a more shaggy form of the brownie but can change their size. Their coloring is all shades of brown. They can appear as a dark blob or just an evil face with a wide nasty grin; their eyes glitter with malice. They are most active and strongest at night. They like to cause nightmares, hide things, blow dirt into people's eyes, and creep close behind people in frightening situations. They easily communicate with flies, mosquitoes, wasps, and hornets, sending out calls that cause swarms of these insects to attack or annoy warm-blooded creatures, particularly humans.

Fortunately, goblins do not have permanent homes but move from place to place in gangs. They take shelter in deserted houses, old ruins, clefts in rocks, and the twisting roots of old trees. If you hear high-pitched squeals and shrill tittering at night, there is a goblin gang close by.

Magickal Uses: Do not contact goblins at all!

Personality Traits: A person who enjoys frightening, humiliating, and terrorizing others.

Gremlins

Many people think gremlins only surfaced during World War II, when strange problems began occurring with airplanes, but this is not the case. These troublesome creatures have been around as long as humans have. In the beginning, their relationship with humans was a good one—the gremlins shared new inventions, helped make more efficient tools, and inspired people to become proficient craftsmen. However, as soon as humans began to take full credit for these improvements, the gremlins took offense and refused to help any longer. Now, they enjoy doing little annoying things to make the lives of humans miserable. They like to choke off the fuel to the lawnmower, play with the hot and cold water to the shower, cause paint to run down your arm, and make the toast burn by holding down the lever. They never run out of ways to torment. Since they like machinery of all kinds, there is at least one gremlin in every home and business.

Magickal Uses: Not recommended.

Personality Traits: A person who prefers working with inventions and machinery to socializing with people. May be cranky and a loner.

Green Man

This woodland entity is known by many names, depending upon the area and culture. To the Celts, he was Cernunnos, Lord of the Forest and Animals. In Old Welsh he was called Arddhu (the Dark One), Atho, or the Horned God. People of the English countryside knew him merely as the Green Man.

These faery-connected forest dwellers have a green human form and wear scanty outfits of various leaves. Their primary task is to care for the groves and woodlands, even single trees upon occasion. Shy but friendly toward humans, the Green Men only give problems to woodcutters or gamekeepers who show no respect for nature.

In Germany and parts of Scandinavia, similar beings are called the Oak Men. These guard the groves of sacred oak trees. They are not friendly to humans at all but rarely cause them trouble.

Scotland and Cornwall are inhabited by short, thin creatures called the Brown Men or Moor Men. These beings dress in brown foliage and have coppery red hair. They avoid humans whenever possible and take their job as protector and nurturer of moor animal life quite seriously.

Magickal Uses: Making connections with nature and Earth energies. Linking with the faery side of the planet.

Personality Traits: One who prefers to live in or near vast woodlands and does not care for city life. A loner who communes with nature through photography, painting, or the study of wildlife.

Kelpies

This is another faery creature that is found near water. In Scotland, it is called the kelpie, while in Cornwall it is known as the *shoney*. Although it can appear as a human or a seal, it usually takes the form of a white horse with a foamy mane. The kelpie wails loudly just before a storm. In semihuman form, the kelpie looks hairy with seaweed hair.

The kelpie likes to hide in bushes near a loch or sea, waiting for a human on horseback to come by. It then leaps behind the rider, trapping him or her in a crushing grip with its long arms, while spooking the horse until the rider loses control. When the kelpie tires of this malicious game, it leaps back into the water.

Magickal Uses: Not recommended; dangerous.

Personality Traits: One who plays with the emotions of others, then discards them without a thought. People who engage in harmful practical jokes.

Knockers

These creatures of the mines may have come to Cornwall with the Phoenicians, who long ago traveled to that area to barter for tin, silver, copper, and lead. Although knockers originally habitated only in Cornwall, they have made their way to Australia, where they are called knackers. The few miners who have seen these subterranean beings say they resemble gnomes.

Knockers are very helpful to miners. They warn of dangers or often direct them toward a deposit of whatever ore or gems they are seeking. They have also led searchers to trapped miners. They send their warnings of mine collapse, explosion, or flooding in the form of a wild flurry of knockings, hence their name. The miners who respect these creatures will not return to the pits or shafts after such a warning. Neither will they whistle, swear, or make the sign of the cross while in the mines, as these behaviors are repellant to the knockers.

Magickal Uses: Useful in learning to identify and work with metals and gems.

Personality Traits: One who has learned to dig for spiritual treasure deep within the subconscious mind.

Kobolds

Although rarely seen, these beings reportedly look like small old men with wrinkled faces, who wear brown knee pants, red hats, and smoke a pipe. There are two types of kobolds: those who are friendly to humans and those who are troublemakers. If you can entice a friendly kobold into your home, consider yourself very fortunate. If you find yourself with an unfriendly kobold in your house, you should make every effort to remove him. If he feels insulted or ignored, there's a good chance he'll make you trip or burn your fingers. He will also throw things about the house.

In Finland, these creatures are called the *para*. The Finnish say they are more likely to create mischief than anything else, so they make pacts with the *paras*. They offer food and shelter in return for prosperity for the family. However, once invited in, *para* are extremely difficult to evict. For many years, Finnish churches kept special exorcists who did nothing but rid unwanted *paras* from the church.

In Germany, the kobolds are known to the miners as goblins. They live in the mines and, if treated with disrespect, will poison the air or ore in the mine.

Magickal Uses: Unless you are an experienced magician and know which type of kobold you are contacting, it is wiser to leave them alone. If you make connections with a friendly one, he will bring you good luck.

Personality Traits: A person who often takes offense at imagined slights.

Leshy or Leshi

The two varieties of this being are both found in the Slavic-Russian areas. The woodland variety has human bodies, but the horns, ears, and legs of a goat. These forest guardians are primarily active from dusk until dawn during the spring and summer months. Foresters and the few other humans who have seen them say they are very thin and have blue skin and green hair and eyes. Some of them are very dangerous; others only try to frighten humans who enter their domain.

Another type of *leshy* haunts the water and its immediate surrounding area. They try to push humans into the water, hoping they will drown.

Magickal Uses: Too unpredictable and dangerous to work with.

Personality Traits: One who uses a supposed love of nature to cause harm to others.

Merfolk

Generally known as mermaids and mermen, these beings live in the oceans of the world. They have a human upper body, but the iridescent, scaly tale of a great fish from the navel downward. Most of them can cast aside their tail for a short time and walk along the beaches like humans. The Irish equivalent is the *merrow,* who wears a red cap and whose appearance heralds a storm.

They have been known to intermarry with humans, just as the faeries do. However, marriage to the merfolk lasts only a short time before they disappear once more into the ocean. The offspring of these unions have webs between their toes.

Some of the merfolk have been known to grant wishes and give humans psychic powers.

Magickal Uses: When doing spells for freedom, imagination, inspiration, foretelling, or finding hidden treasure.

Personality Traits: A person with such controlled emotions that he or she rarely makes or keeps a relationship commitment. One who tries to help people with troubled emotions.

Ohdows

Part of the Native American culture, these mysterious, very small tribal creatures live underground and are very rarely seen. They are not deformed in any manner, but simply a tiny, perfect version of members of the Indian tribes.

The *ohdows* have great magickal powers, which they use to help humans, animals, and the earth itself. Their main goal is to keep control of gigantic evil spirits that live deep inside the planet. These evil spirits constantly try to get loose from their subterranean prisons so they can destroy everything on Earth. Sometimes one can hear them beating on the stone walls of underground caverns, making terrifying noises and rumblings. This activity will last until the *ohdows* once more gain control over them.

Magickal Uses: Protection from natural disasters, such as earthquakes, eruptions, and tsunami.

Personality Traits: A person who is able to predict future disasters.

Pegasus

This horse of ancient Greek tales is white with golden wings and the ability to fly into any realm it wishes. Said to be an offspring of the fierce Medusa, Pegasus is immortal and has direct connections with the Muses. The opposite of its mother in temperament, Pegasus is graceful, beautiful, gentle, and wise.

Magickal Uses: Traveling in the astral world from one realm to another. Gaining skill and inspiration in the arts. Changing negative energy into positive energy.

Personality Traits: A person who tries to help everyone. One who is skilled in the arts and/or astral travel.

Pixies

No one knows where pixies originated, only that they suddenly appeared in the far western sections of England, especially Cornwall. For a reason not known to humans, there has always been a feud between pixies and the Small Folk.

The word pesky is derived from pixie and aptly describes their activities. Although not dangerous to humans, they are malicious and tricky, particularly when it comes to misleading travelers. In Cornwall, this is known as being "pixie-led." Tradition says the only remedy is to put your coat on inside out; this breaks the pixie spell. Farmers who live in country inhabited by pixies try to stay on their good side by leaving out water for the mothers to wash their babies in and by keeping the hearth clean for their dances.

Pixies are about as tall as a human hand is long, but they can expand their bodies to human size. They are easily differentiated from other faery kin by their bright red hair, green eyes, pointed ears, and up-turned noses. They prefer to wear tight-fitting green outfits, which serve as camouflage when they are in the fields and forests. Sometimes they will wear a toadstool or a foxglove blossom as a hat—these are two plants they especially love. They also like to spend their time relaxing or playing in flower gardens and herb beds.

Although both males and females can present themselves as humans, it is usually the males who do this. So if you see or meet someone who matches the pixie description and has a mischievous smile, it is best to avoid becoming involved with them.

Magickal Uses: Work with pixies only if you are a very experienced magician, or your magickal work will likely turn chaotic.

Personality Traits: A person with a sense of humor who is malicious and hurtful to others.

Pookas, Puca, and Puck

This being is found in the woodlands and looks similar to a pixie, with its pointed ears and close-fitting green suit. A close friend of the Small Folk, the shape-shifting *puca* of England plays a willow twig flute for moonlight dances. The English type likes humans as long as he is treated with respect, but he will harass anyone who scorns their lover. He tends to all the animals and plants of the meadows and forests.

The Welsh *pwca* ("pooka"), however, is very ill-tempered and ugly. It dislikes humans and is quarrelsome even with its own kind. This is the only *pooka* known to enter human houses.

The Kornbockes of Scandinavia and Germany are *pookas* that resemble fauns, with goat horns and hind legs. Although they help grow the grain, they will make it unusable if they can. In the Old German, they were known as *Putz* or *Butz*. The *puki* of Iceland is considered an evil spirit.

The Irish *phouka* is a human-shaped creature that can shape-shift into a horse. It hangs around remote, lonely areas, such as bogs and swamps. Seeing one is thought to be a bad omen. Riding one in its horse form is very foolish, for you will not be able to dismount until the *phouka* allows it.

Magickal Uses: Although Puck is mischievous, he can be very helpful in learning the flute or working with the energy of wild animals. Though his humor is usually gentle, he will spare nothing to punish wayward lovers.

Personality Traits: A person who has a dry sense of humor and likes to play tricks on others. One who is close to the earth and all nature. Rarely accepts responsibility for his mischievous pranks.

Red Cap

This evil creature lives only on the border between England and Scotland, where he inhabits ruined castles and watchtowers. If such places aren't available, he will take up residence in piles of old stones. One of the most dangerous of the faery kin, avoid the Red Cap at all times, for he seeks human blood to keep his cap colored bright red.

He looks like a small old man with fiery red eyes and long gray hair. Although he wears iron boots, he moves swiftly and can overtake any human he sees. Instead of hands, he has eagle claws.

Magickal Uses: Do not contact or work with the Red Cap. Extremely dangerous.

Personality Traits: A person who constantly seeks out potential victims, either of the emotions or the body.

Ribhaus

These beings, all male, are the elves of India. They are said to be the sons of Indra by Saranyu. They are artisans who are concerned with good crops, herbs, streams, and creativity in general.

Magickal Uses: Learning about herbs and gardening. Seeking creativity.

Personality Traits: A person who loves to garden and is concerned with the soil.

Selkies

The seas around the Faroe Islands of Britain are the home of the *selkies,* or Seal-People. They have a true human form, but wear seal skins when traveling from one place to another. Every ninth night, tradition says, they dance in human form on the beaches. They live in underwater worlds that are enclosed in gigantic air bubbles.

Their beauty and large liquid-looking eyes make them very attractive to humans. The males frequently have affairs with human women but never stay long. The offspring of these unions have webs between their toes, just as human children of the merfolk do.

Magickal Uses: Treat with respect. Useful when traveling into astral water realms.

Personality Traits: People who live their lives as they want, not influenced by fads, fashion, or the opinions of others.

Trolls

Originally, the trolls inhabited the Scandinavian countries and northern Germany. However, like many other astral creatures, they are now found around the world. In Sweden, they are known as *trolds*; in Denmark they are called Hill Men or Berg Men.

Trolls come in all shapes and sizes, from small to giant, very thin to stocky. However, all are rather indistinct in shape and stone-colored and have barely any neck. They are very strong, and most of them are not intelligent. A few are quite skilled, however, at mechanics and blacksmithing.

Although trolls prefer to live in the mountains or deep forests, underground, or in dark, enclosed places, some of them have migrated into towns and cities to live among humans. These emigrants are spotted under highway overpasses, in storm drains, and in abandoned concrete buildings. Even the smallest hill is home to a troll.

They prefer to go out at night, as they do not like sunlight. Old tales say sunlight turns them into stone. Since they can become invisible at night, it is difficult to see a troll.

Trolls tend to run in gangs that bully others. They throw stones at humans, because to trolls humans smell bad and look ugly. Scandinavian folklore tells stories of trolls stealing children and attacking people who are abroad at night. If they come too close to farms, the cats and dogs will hide and the cows won't give milk.

In Iceland, a branch of the troll family is called the *illes* ("eels"). They also live underground and come out only at night. Although their true form is hairy and dark-colored, the *illes* can shape-shift into attractive human forms. They dance, sing, and play beautiful music under the full moon, in their attempt to lure humans into their underground homes.

The Hollow Men or *Foddenskkmaend* (Underground People) are the names given to trolls on the Faroe Islands. The island inhabitants are also afraid of trolls, for they believe these creatures kidnap humans and keep them in their hill homes.

Magickal Uses: One must take care in working with trolls, for they can be troublesome, even dangerous at times. If you establish an amiable relationship with trolls, without commanding them, they can teach you how to draw upon the great energies of mountains.

Personality Traits: A strong person who subscribes to the martial arts in order to defend the helpless. If a negative personality trait, one who uses physical strength to bully.

Uldra or Huldra-Folk

Although the Huldra-Folk have some characteristics of elves, dwarves, and trolls, the Laplanders clearly separate this species of faery kin from all others. The Lapps also call them the *uldra,* and they say they are gentle nature beings of the far northern areas of their migratory paths. Although they live underground, the *uldra* frequently come out in winter to search for hibernating animals such as bears. Adults are rarely seen, but the curious *uldra* children, who are covered with black hair and have sharp teeth, sometimes wander into a Lapp camp.

However, in Norway these beings are called the *Huldra-Folk, Hogfolk* (Hill-People), or *Bjergfolk.* They live in family clans in caves and small hills, have the ability to become invisible or shape-shift, and can predict the future or cast spells for prosperity. Their hill homes are said to be decorated with gold and crystal. Usually friendly toward humans, the *uldra* or *Huldra-Folk* greatly dislike the sound of bells.

In Norway and other Scandinavian countries (outside of Lapland), these beings are believed to be very beautiful and quite skilled at singing and playing music. A few elderly fiddlers know one of their tunes, "The Elf-King's Tune," but they refuse to play it. Once a fiddler starts, he can't stop until someone cuts the strings on his instrument.

Magickal Uses: Learning how to shape-shift or become invisible. Prosperity, music, singing.

Personality Traits: One who prefers solitude and nature to the busy city life.

Unicorn

Although unicorns tend to shun humans, they have always been associated with faeries, elves, and elemental spirits, particularly those of the woodlands.

The physical description of the unicorn varies from culture to culture. The European description is most familiar because of ancient tapestries and tales. It is said that the European unicorn has the head and body of a horse, the hind legs of a stag, the tail of a lion, and a long, spiral, twisted horn in the center of its forehead. It also has cloven hooves. It is a pure white with blue eyes; the horn is a pale ivory tint.

Untamed, with very strong elemental powers, the unicorn is a symbol of transformation through destruction, or the breaking down of certain events or traits, so that a new life and cycle can begin.

Meeting and riding a unicorn during meditation or astral travel is an important event. A unicorn is capable of taking you on dimensional journeys through time and space to show you what is needed to make positive changes in your physical and spiritual life.

Magickal Uses: Working with unicorns can have a powerful effect on your spiritual growth. If one appears unexpectedly, consider it a warning of the profound changes about to occur in your life: good fortune, prosperity, a positive change in ethics, unlimited individual power.

Personality Traits: A person who quietly works to improve her or his spiritual growth and helps others, if possible.

Urisk or Uruisg

This Scottish brownie is a solitary creature who is half human and half goat. It ordinarily makes its home around lonely pools but will sometimes reside near a house. If an *urisk* lives nearby, consider it very lucky. Though the *urisk* prefers to live alone, he gathers with others to celebrate the solstice and equinox.

Magickal Uses: Call upon this helpful creature when working to heal animals or grow a garden.

Personality Traits: One who has an unusual connection with animals and plants.

Wild Women

The *Wilde Frauen* (Wild Women) of Germany seem to be related in some manner to the elves. These beautiful women have long flowing hair and live inside the Wunderberg (or Underberg), a huge mountain on the moor near Salzburg. The Wunderberg is believed to be hollow inside and filled with springs, gardens, palaces, and special sacred areas—all for the Wild Women. No one has ever seen males accompanying them.

Magickal Uses: Women should call upon these beings only for help in becoming independent and accomplishing goals.

Personality Traits: A woman who is perfectly comfortable without any male companionship. One who does not particularly like men.

Chapter 14

The Secret Faery Oracle

The Faery Oracle is an amazing divination tool that you can use during meditation or spellwork. It is easy to remember the meanings of the stones used because of the symbols. These symbols are easily understood by the Fay and elves, for they are the members of Faery Land who will help you understand the significance of these stones.

To make your own Faery Oracle stones, I suggest you purchase the flat, clear or colored stones sold in craft stores for decoration. If you are determined to make a "natural" set, you can search for twenty flat stones that are about the same size, out in nature. This will take you much longer, and the stones will be heavier than the ones sold in craft stores. Also, make or purchase a bag with a drawstring to keep your stones in.

If using the oracle in meditation, choose a stone or stones that symbolize what you want to learn on your journey. When using the oracle for spellwork, pick out the stone or stones that correspond to the spell you will be doing. And remember, do not do spellwork to harm or control others. The faeries will not like their oracle used in this manner and will cause you problems if you do so.

You may wish to draw one stone each morning as a guide for the learning of that day. Or, you can draw three stones with a specific question in mind, laying them in a horizontal line. The first stone represents the event or problem about which you asked. The second stone is what will happen if you take no action. The third stone symbolizes what will happen if you take action.

Before each "learning" (which is what the faeries call a reading), you may wish to burn a green candle and use the following chant to attract faeries:

Faeries, show the truth to me.
For only truth I wish to see.

- **Leaf:** Small things leading to larger events; new beginnings.
- **Flower:** Romance, love, relationship, friendship.
- **Tree:** Strength, standing firm, someone who will shelter and protect you.
- **Sun:** Happiness, prosperity, good health.
- **Moon:** Truth not completely revealed; uncover all details before making a decision.
- **Stars:** Spiritual growth, the beginning of another cycle in your life, special guidance from Faery Land.
- **Sword:** Beware of enemies; protect yourself at all times.
- **River:** Movement.
- **Mountain:** Obstacles, challenges.
- **Clouds:** Small negative happenings annoy you; an unhappy spot in an otherwise positive day.
- **Archway:** Good luck comes your way; new opportunities arise.
- **Wand:** Magickal energy is available for your use; by directing your focused energy into a project, you can complete it right away.
- **White feather, upright:** Very positive energy that overrides any negative stones and adds power to the positive ones.
- **Black feather, downward:** Very negative energy that overrides whatever positive stone it is next to.

- **Key:** You have been wondering about an event, job, or person; information will come to you that will act as a key in getting to the truth.
- **Closed door:** The way ahead is blocked; choose another path.
- **Harp:** It is time for you to have joy in your life; take a vacation and have fun.
- **Boat:** Short or long journeys; these can be of a physical, mental, emotional, or spiritual nature.
- **Open treasure chest:** Unexpected money will come your way, either through a new job, a raise, a gift, or an inheritance. This may also mean unexpected expenses.
- **Arrow:** Concentrate on your goals in order to reach them; choose a new goal (target) as soon as you have finished one; keep negative people at a distance.

Chapter 15

Faery Gardens

Before you plant a garden to attract faeries, you need to consider what kinds of faeries inhabit your area. You want, primarily, to greet those faeries first before you invite other faeries to your home.

To increase the faeries' delight in your garden, add shiny marble or agate to parts of your faery paths, perhaps just under an arched trellis or other form you plan to use as a gateway to see into Faery Land.

Faeries not only use mirrors and shining surface as means of transporting themselves from one place to another, they also like to look at their reflections in them. Shiny Victorian-style gazing balls are wonderful additions. The gazing balls not only add visible beauty and interest to even the smallest garden, they also provide the faeries with pleasure. Small mirrors or pieces of mirrors placed next to fountains in shady areas also add interest.

Gardens do not have to be huge to attract faeries. You can grow pots of flowers and herbs on your deck or inside your house, beside a sunny window.

If you use containers for gardening, you will need several large pots with saucers to catch any overflow of water. It is best to use potting soil with vermiculite in it rather than topsoil. Plants need a looser soil to be able to send out new roots easily. Potting soil will not get as hard as topsoil or pack down as tight. You may also want to add a thin layer of large gravel or small pebbles in the bottom of each container. This aids drainage, keeping the plant roots from standing in too much water and rotting.

You can also plant a faery garden in a terrarium. Be certain to choose small plants that require a lot of moisture.

Whether planting an indoor or outdoor garden, read up on any plants you decide to grow and see what type of light they can handle. Some plants will die in full sunlight, but flourish in the shade. Some love and thrive in hot sunlight.

When planning an outdoor garden, it is best to work it out on paper first. This way you can determine where to put the trees and plants you've chosen. Be very certain these plants can survive in your region. You can plant for color or variety, for instance, you might want a small section of your garden to have all red or blue flowers. Check the height to which the flowers will grow, so you can plant the tallest ones in the back of the flowerbed and the shortest in the front. If you have chain-link fencing around your yard, you can plant grapes or vining plants next to it. By coaxing the running vines along the fence, you provide a colorful screen. Two good flowering plants for this are the trumpet vine, blooming in red or yellow, and wisteria.

If you can include an arched trellis at the garden entrance, by all means do so. Line the space under the arch with marble chips, and use it as a gateway to the outer edges of Faery Land. Have chairs and benches set in shady, secluded spots to use for meditation and as an invitation to the Fay to relax and enjoy your garden with you.

You can add concrete stepping stones or white marble chips for paths. Place a stepping stone set in the middle of the flowerbed so you can step on it to reach the back, rather than compressing the dirt by walking on it. If you are fortunate to have, or find, pieces of natural shiny rocks, you can use them to draw attention to a certain area. It is also nice to have a small weathervane or sundial. Faeries also like humans to include bird feeders and birdbaths, so their feathered friends are cared for.

You can also attract faeries by placing little statues in among the plants, inside or out. A wide variety of such garden items are now available, from large mushrooms to gazing balls, faery statues, even Quan Yin and Buddha. If you do not have electricity available to run a small fountain, look for one that runs off a solar panel.

The flowers and trees in the following list are only a small sampling of the traditional faery plants. As you know by now, all plants are attended by faeries, whether the flowers and plants are domesticated or wild. A wider variety of flowers in your garden will encourage the Small Folk to frequent your area in large numbers. Some of these faeries may be foreign ones, who came to this country when their plants were brought in years ago.

Faery Flowers

Bay Laurel: This tree attracts friendly faeries and repels unfriendly ones. Burn a tiny pinch of dried bay leaf to open a gateway into Faery Land.

Bluebells: These are a favorite flower of the faeries. Sit near blooming bluebells at noon. Soon you will sense faeries all around you. British tales say that the ringing of bluebells summons faeries to their midnight dances.

Clover: All types of clover are considered sacred to the faeries, especially the beautiful red clover.

Cowslip: This flower is believed to help faeries become invisible.

Daisy: When out seeking faeries, wearing a chain of daisies around your head will protect you against their tricks and pranks.

Fern: Ferns and faeries have gone together for centuries. Tradition says that if you sit near a fern bed at night, you will entice faeries to you.

Foxglove: This flowering plant is also called Faery Fingers, named for the tiny finger-size spots on the flowers. However, the plant and seeds are poisonous because they contain digitalis, a powerful medicinal. Some of the Small Folk use the flowers for summer hats and gloves.

Heather: This plant attracts faeries and elves.

Hollyhock: The buds are used in faery potions and ointments.

Jasmine: Faeries from India, China, and Arabia adore this scent and will go wherever the plant grows. Jasmine incense or tea helps some people reach an astral-level trance.

Lilac: Faeries are very attracted to the odor of these flowers, and they make wine from them.

Marigold: The buds are used in some faery ointments. Take a marigold blossom, soak it for six hours in clear spring water, then dab this mixture onto your eyelids. This will help make the faeries visible.

Mugwort: This herb is often used in dream pillows or, when dried, as incense in spells to help you contact Faery Land.

Pansy: The faeries use this flower to make a very powerful love potion, though they have never revealed the secret recipe to humans. They will, however, sometimes use this potion to make humans fall in love.

Peony: The flowers of this plant repel unfriendly faeries and attract those of Oriental origin.

Poppy: Use the seeds as a topping on faery cakes. Poppy flowers in a garden also attract faeries.

Primrose: These attract faeries; however, tend them well or you will have ill luck. Growing this flower near your front door makes it easier for the Small Folk to enter your home and bless you while you sleep. Primrose is also believed to help faeries remain invisible.

Pussywillow: All kinds of the Small Folk use the silky, soft catkin pods as pillows. Planting pussywillow in your garden will attract many faeries.

Rosemary: Grow this protective plant to attract the attention of elves and friendly faeries.

Strawberry: Faeries adore strawberries. Burn the incense indoors to attract them and leave an offering of the berries out at night.

Thyme: The buds are used in faery ointments. Faeries love the scent, so carry a piece of thyme to help you see faeries.

Vervain: This was always a very sacred, protective plant to the Celts. It is also loved by faeries. Use a little in your bathwater to induce dreams about Faery Land.

Faery Trees

Ash: Tradition says that this was the most sacred tree of the Norse peoples and well loved by the elves. It is one of the triad of faery trees; the other two are hawthorn and oak.

Birch: Among the Norse and Celtic peoples, this tree was said to symbolize birthing and new beginnings.

Bonsai: These carefully manicured miniature trees are favorites with Japanese faeries.

Elder: Elderberry wine is sometimes called faery wine. This tree protects the elves and faeries, and they in turn take care of the tree. It is also connected with the Nordic spirit, the Old Lady of the Elder.

Hawthorn: A faery favorite that blooms near the first of May, this tree cannot be cut without asking permission from the tree spirit and pouring a gift of milk and honey near the roots. These bushes also protect against any psychic trouble sent your way. One of the triad of faery trees; the other two are ash and oak.

Hazel: Some faeries weave the leaves into their clothing, and they all love the hazelnuts.

Oak: Elves and the Fay in particular can always be found beside the oldest oaks in a grove of trees. One of the triad of faery trees; the other two are ash and hawthorn.

Rowan: This tree protects against all malicious spirits. Faeries love rowan jelly.

Willow: Faeries love to sing and inspire poets who sit under willows. They also use its twigs for wands.

Faery Stones

Although faeries are especially fond of crystal in all its forms, they also love the shiny, smooth stones you can buy at rock shops. Faeries are closely connected with marble, tiger's eye, staurolite, obsidian, fluorite, peridot, and jade. However, their most sacred and favored stone is the emerald.

Garden Welcome

You may have planted the most beautiful garden in the world, filling it with faery flowers, trees, stones, and fountains, but the faeries will not feel welcome to stay and live there until you issue a formal invitation. The best way to do so is to recite a chant and proceed to have a party, offering ginger cookies, little cakes, chamomile tea, and other drinks set out on a table with a cloth. You can hold this party on your porch, in your gazebo, or under the shade of a tree. The place is not as important as the invitation.

The chant you may use is this:

See this garden made for you?
O Faery Folk, all friends so true.
Welcome here to live all time,
For this is yours and also mine.
Bless the plants and bless the soil.
Bless all those who in here toil.
Bless the wild things that come and go.
Your presence will make this garden grow.
Welcome!

Chapter 16

Faery Houses and Sacred Places

Honoring the faeries with little houses, either inside or outside your home, is certain to attract a large number of various kinds of faeries. The Small Folk are curious about such things. Besides, it is a lot of fun for adults and children to construct these houses. They can be very simple or very elaborate, depending upon the time, money, and space you have—and, of course, your talents, if you intend to construct an elaborate house from boards instead of a kit.

The simplest and most natural faery house is one made from material you find on a walk through the forest. You can build one of these little houses right there in the forest and leave it for the faeries to find and enjoy.

Never break limbs off trees or remove the bark, as the faeries will consider this a negative act to their plant. Instead, use only the cast-off natural materials you find on the forest floor.

Begin by gathering cones. The size depends upon what is available in the area and how large you want the house to be. Lean these, one by one, against a tree or rock to make two walls, parallel to each other. Now lay pieces of bark or clusters of pine needles across these cones to make a roof. You can either clear a little path up to the house or create one with tiny rocks. If you leave a friendship offering for the faeries, place it outside the house.

Tiny decorative birdhouses also make good faery homes. Make certain the hole is too small for real birds to enter. If the birdhouse is a wooden one, you can decorate the outside by gluing tiny artificial flowers and/or vines to it. Then paint "Welcome" or "Faery House" above the tiny, round opening. You can hang this inside or out.

Another cute indoor faery house is made out of a bird cage, artificial green vines, a clip-on butterfly or two, and a few bright artificial flowers. If you are using an old bird cage, be certain to clean it very well before beginning its transformation. You can buy small wooden bird cages that are excellent for making this type of faery home.

Play with the vines by draping and wrapping them around the cage in different ways until you find a design you like. Make certain the door is open and nothing will cover it. Using a hot glue gun, carefully attach the vines around the cage in the design you choose. Decide where you want to place the flowers and glue them into place as well. Clip the butterfly on the cage near the cage's top or close to the door. Let the cage stand overnight to be certain everything will stay in place.

Now comes the interesting part: decorating the inside. Since everything you put inside must go through the cage door, remember to keep your decorative items small. Many of your items can be handmade or bought in a miniature shop that sells supplies for dollhouses.

Spread a nice rug or pretty piece of material used as a rug across the floor. For chairs, use the tops of perfume bottles or other tall bottle tops. You can decorate these by gluing pieces of furlike cloth or shiny satin around and over the top of the cap. To complete the chair, cut rectangular pieces of cardboard for the chair backs. Paint them with a color that matches the chair fabric. When these are dry, glue the cardboard to the cap to make the chair back. Put the chairs (however many you've made) on the center of the rug. You can easily make pillows by sewing little three-sided pockets of fabric, stuffing these with cotton balls, and sewing them closed.

Let the faeries inspire your imagination. Pictures can be made by gluing a magazine cutout onto cardboard and fastening this to bars of the cage. A tiny vase of small artificial flowers can add interest near one of the chairs. Some dollhouse furniture will fit nicely through the door, but measure carefully before buying. What looks as if it will go through easily often doesn't.

The small, lightweight dollhouse kits make wonderful faery houses and give you more space to decorate and arrange things. Lay out all the pieces of the kit to be sure you have everything. Read the instructions; putting the house together in a certain way makes sense and prevents mistakes. After constructing the dollhouse according to the manufacturer's instructions (this won't be hard to do), let it stand for a day or two before going on with your work. You can then paint the dollhouse, inside and out, or paint the outside and use dollhouse wallpaper on the inside.

You can go extravagant and unusual when decorating faery houses, for faeries love bright colors and creative things. Cover the roof with moss from a craft store. Use rubber stamps and bright inks to make patterns on the walls, inside and out. Put an artificial cobweb in a corner of one room.

Faeries enjoy soft and shiny things. Make certain the bed and chairs are soft and cushy. Hang shiny draperies from the ceiling in the dancing rooms.

Remember, this is a faery house, not a dollhouse. Think like a faery. What rooms would a faery want? Certainly not a kitchen, for they gather their food from nature itself. A dining room, perhaps. And certainly a room or two for dancing. Maybe a small room with a little bed for taking naps when they aren't sleeping with their plants. Faeries bathe in the rain and dew, so they have no use for a bathroom. However, the faeries might appreciate a dressing room with a mirror where they can try on different clothes when preparing for a dance or celebration.

Provide small tables on which you can place tiny glasses and cups. Brighten the rooms with vases of different types of artificial flowers, mirrors, and pictures. If you choose to have a dining room, decorate the table with a runner of lace and a floral bouquet in the center. You can even make dinner dishes out of clay or purchase them. The small dressing room should have a mirror and perhaps a tiny vanity so the faeries can dust their faces with pollen to make themselves pretty.

With a dollhouse as a faery house, you can redecorate for the changing seasons of the year. In autumn you might string a cluster of tiny, colorful leaves in each room, along with acorns and bundles of grass to look like cornstalks. At the winter solstice, you can place a fir tree in one of the dancing rooms, complete with tiny decorations and lights, and presents beneath the tree. You can also hang sparkling snowflakes from the ceilings of each room. In the spring, set tiny pots of flowers in groups in the dancing rooms to celebrate the new growth. For summer, you can make fruit and vegetables out of clay or purchase them ready made. Put these in bowls on the dining table and on the stands in the dancing rooms.

If you have the time and money, you can make your faery house into a faery castle. You can install lighting in each room, with beautiful chandeliers in the dancing rooms. You can purchase small musical instruments for their dances. You can even buy fancy rugs for the floors—look for those with Persian and Oriental patterns.

If you have the space, you can create an adjoining lawn and deck area for the faery house. It is possible to add a barbecue, hot tub, colorful plants, and miniature trees, as well as a small pond made of aluminum foil or a small mirror.

If you live near a miniatures store, you can see firsthand all the possibilities for decorating the house. Also, do not neglect flea markets and yard sales, for you never know what you will find to create something for your special house.

Let your creativity run free. This will strengthen it and attract more faery inspiration to you. This, in turn, will strengthen your friendship bond with the faeries.

Remember to think like a faery when making a faery house, and ask for faery help!

Faery House Welcoming Ritual

Whatever kind of faery house you have made, a faery or faery family will be happy to move in. Sprinkle a little ground ginger before the entrance to show that faeries are particularly welcome there. If this is a permanent outdoor structure, plant both early spring and late summer flowers around it, both to hide it from view and to make it beautiful. If it is an indoor structure, you can buy well-made artificial flowers and set them around the structure.

However, you must send out a welcoming call, indoors or outdoors, to notify the faeries that a house is ready to be occupied. Use this chant:

> The house is built, the door open wide,
> O faeries, come and look inside.

Clap your hands three times.

> Magick of the sun and moon
> Will call a dweller very soon.

Clap your hands three times.

> True friendship I send to Faery Folk.
> May this house be full of the Small Folk.

Clap your hands three times.

Now walk away, giving the faeries the privacy to look over the house and choose which type of faery will live in it. And know in your heart that your garden, your home, and your faery house are now filled with your wonderful friends.

Chapter 17

Stories for Adults and Children

The Wizard and the Spring Maiden
(Imbolc—February 2)

The winter snows still lay thick over the frozen ground, as the cold wind whistled through the bare limbs of the trees. Even the new Sun felt cold to the little birds that huddled together in the trees to keep warm.

"The wizard isn't awake yet, is he?" asked a tiny chickadee.

"No, the door to his house is still closed and locked." A bluejay cocked her head and stared down at the little hill in the meadow below. "I haven't seen so much as a hair of his beard at the window either."

"I wish the Maiden would awake. Then we would know spring will soon arrive." The chickadee fluffed its feathers as it looked off across the snow-covered fields.

A gray squirrel suddenly poked his head out of a hole in the tree and chattered at the birds in a grumbling voice. "What is all the noise out here?" he asked. "I'm trying to sleep, you silly birds!"

"The wizards is still asleep, and the Maiden hasn't awakened yet," the chickadees answered all at one time.

"Perhaps there will be no spring this year." The blue jay flew to a limb nearer the squirrel and looked at him with her black eyes.

"Nonsense," the squirrel answered as he squeezed out of his hole to sit on the bare branch. "Spring always comes." He rubbed the sleep from his eyes, then fluffed his tail with his little paws.

"We're so hungry," chirped the chickadees. "If the Maiden doesn't wake up soon, we will starve."

The squirrel cocked his head, listening for the sweet song of the Maiden as She calls everything in the land to begin waking up. He heard nothing but the whistle of the cold wind and the rattle of the bare tree branches. In the meadow just beyond the wizard's hill, he saw a flock of sheep and heard their bleating, but he saw no baby lambs.

"This is the right time of year for the Maiden to awake and the young Sun King to dance through our forest," the squirrel said. He scratched his head as he thought. "I'll go wake the wizard and ask him if he knows why the Maiden still sleeps."

The squirrel dashed down the tree trunk and leaped across the snow. In long leaps, he ran across the ground until he reached the rocks surrounding the hidden door to the wizard's home. He stopped and listened, but he heard no movement within the hill house.

"Wake up! Wake up, wizard!" The squirrel pounded on the door. "Sleepy old wizard," he grumbled to himself. "Wake up, you lazy gnome! We need your help." He pounded again on the door with both paws.

Green Leaf, the little gnome wizard, stirred restlessly in his downy bed. Someone was pounding on his door, making a terrible racket that echoed through the rooms and halls of his snug little hill house. He opened one eye and looked around the room.

One beam of pale sunlight crept through a crack in the shutters over the windows and lit up the face of the strange clock beside the wizard's bed. Instead of hours and minutes, the clock face had the names of the seasonal festivals: Imbolc, Spring Equinox, Beltane, Summer Solstice, Lunasa, Autumn Equinox, Samhain, and Winter Solstice.

Green Leaf yawned, then opened both eyes to stare at the clock. "It's Imbolc!" he said, as he sat up suddenly in bed. "I've overslept. Oh my, oh my."

The little gnome wizard scrambled out of his warm nest of blankets and hurriedly dressed. The pounding on his door kept banging through the hill house.

"I'm coming," Green Leaf shouted as he hopped toward the door, pulling on his boots. He fumbled with the lock, finally opening the little door. "Stop that noise!" he said as the squirrel jumped around and chattered at him. "I haven't had my tea yet!"

"No time, no time!" said the squirrel. "The Maiden is still asleep! There are no lambs in the fields! The young Sun King hasn't arrived! Hurry, wizard, hurry!"

Green Leaf sighed as he put on his heavy green cloak and his tall pointed red hat. With his wooden staff in one hand, he trudged out into the snow and headed for the thickest part of the forest. Soon he was deep inside the old forest of bare tree trunks and snow-covered firs and pines. Behind him the pale rays of the Sun began to creep through the trees, as if they followed his tiny footprints in the snow.

"I wish the Maiden would sleep in the same place each year," he grumbled, but he knew She didn't. It was his job each Imbolc to find Her sleeping place and wait there until the young Sun King arrived.

He searched and searched for the sleeping Maiden until he at last found her curled up in the shelter of a hawthorn thicket. She looked so beautiful, her long hair falling down over Her arms, that Green Leaf couldn't be grumpy anymore. He smiled, then raised his arms and began to sing his Imbolc greeting to the Sun King.

The forest suddenly lit up with brilliant sunbeams as the young Sun King danced through the trees toward him. The glow about Him was so bright that Green Leaf had to squint his eyes to see.

"Blessed Imbolc, Green Leaf." The deep voice and loving smile of the Sun King warmed the little gnome wizard.

"Blessed Imbolc, Lord," Green Leaf answered as he bowed to the Sun King. "I thought I was late."

"No, my little friend. Everything in the world knows when Imbolc comes, all the animals and plants and even gnomes." The Sun King's smile lit up the trees around them. "Awake, my Lady," He said, as He knelt to kiss the sleeping Maiden.

The Maiden sat up, stretched Her arms, and smiled. "It is time for all the world to awake," She said, and the Sun King nodded as He helped Her to Her feet. They went off together through the forest, dancing to awaken the life-energy of the Earth.

As Green Leaf trudged back through the snow to his hill home, he could still hear the wake-up song of the Maiden and feel it spreading out through the world. Around him the life-energy in the trees began to stir. Deep in the ground he could feel the little burrowing creatures starting to wake from their winter sleep. New life was stirring all around him. The gnome wizard crossed the meadow where the sheep were and found the first of the newborn wobbly-legged spring lambs blinking in the sunlight.

"Welcome to the world," Green Leaf said to the little lamb. "Soon everything will be wide awake and growing. The grass will be sweet and green. And you will have other little lambs to play with." The lamb and its mother looked at the gnome wizard and blinked their eyes.

"Yes, the life-energy from the Maiden is once more running through the world, making everything new," Green Leaf said, as he tramped down the path to his house. Suddenly, he felt the energy flowing through his own body. He leaped into the air and clicked his heels together in joy. "The Maiden is awake!" he shouted to the squirrel and birds waiting for him near his door.

Green Leaf went back inside his hill home and hung up his cloak and hat. "Now I am going to have a cup of tea, then go back to bed and have a nap until Spring Equinox." And the little gnome wizard did just that.

Spring Equinox
(March)

The little rabbit yawned wide, as he looked out from his burrow at the morning sun on the grass. His brothers and sisters crowded behind him, twitching their whiskers, impatient for him to go outside.

"Oh, do get out of the way, Fluff," said one of his sisters, pushing against him. "You always just sit around and look at everything. We're hungry."

As Fluff hopped out into the spring sunshine, his brothers and sisters rushed past him and began to scamper about, eating the tender, new grass. Fluff nibbled a few leaves, but he was more interested in the strange bright colors he saw among the grass stems over by the edge of the meadow. No one saw him hop away to find out what grass grew in such wonderful colors near the trees.

"What strange grass is this?" Fluff said, as he smelled the brightly colored plants. "And why doesn't my family eat it?"

"It isn't grass, little rabbit, but flowers." The soft, gentle voice startled Fluff, and he jumped back, then looked up to see who was speaking.

A beautiful young woman stood smiling at him. Around her head was a crown made of flowers. Her eyes were the deep blue of the sky just after the sun went down, her hair a rich brown like the leaves left on the oak trees. Fluff could see her bare toes under the edge of her long white gown. In one hand she carried a basket woven out of willow limbs.

"Who are you?" he asked. "You aren't a rabbit."

The lady laughed, and the laughter made Fluff feel safe and warm. "No, little Fluff, I am not a rabbit. I am the Spring Maiden. At this time of year I walk through the forests and meadows, calling to the flowers and plants and trees to drink in the rich sunshine and grow faster. The birds and animals hear me also and begin to plan their nests and soft burrows for the little babies who will soon be born." The lady smiled again. "Do you like my flowers?" She pointed at the bright plants peeping through the grass.

"So these are flowers," Fluff said, as he smelled them. "They are very beautiful, but not as beautiful as you are, Spring Maiden."

The little rabbit jumped back as a small boy timidly peeked out from behind the Spring Maiden. A bright light shone around the boy, so bright that Fluff blinked his eyes.

The Spring Maiden put her hand on the boy's shoulder. "This is the little Sun King," she told Fluff. "I am teaching him about the plants and animals, the turning seasons of the year, so he will be a wise ruler of the Earth and all its inhabitants."

"Can we take Fluff with us, Lady?" the little boy asked, looking up at the Spring Maiden.

"Yes," she answered with a smile. "Fluff will help humans remember the importance of this season."

"Why do we have to remind humans?" the little Sun King asked, as he knelt down to pet Fluff. "They should remember."

"The grown-ups get too busy with other things," answered the Spring Maiden, "so we leave special gifts for the children. When the grown-ups see the gifts, they remember and celebrate this season of the year. They remember that the Goddess loves all Her creatures and creations and cares for them."

Fluff left the meadow with the Spring Maiden and the little Sun King, hopping along through the new grass and spring flowers. Everywhere they went in the forests and meadows and along the little streams, they blessed all the animals and plants and the Earth herself. At last they came to the first houses Fluff had ever seen. There were children playing around the houses.

The Spring Maiden reached into her willow basket and took out a bright red egg. "This egg is a symbol of hope and new life," she said as she placed it into the little Sun King's hand. "Animals and plants always know that the Goddess cares for them, that She always makes spring follow winter and good times follow the bad times. Humans forget and need to be reminded."

"I remember," the Sun King said softly. "No life ever really ends. It is always reborn, just as I was."

The Spring Maiden took the little Sun King's hand and, with Fluff hopping beside them, went out to greet the children. They gave each child a red egg and a spring flower from the Lady's basket. The children all petted Fluff and called him a messenger from the Goddess. As they walked away, Fluff heard the children calling to their parents.

"Mother! Father! Look what the beautiful Lady and a shining boy gave us! And we got to pet the Goddess' special rabbit messenger!"

"Is it Spring Equinox already?" The father looked toward the forest where the Lady stood with Fluff at her feet. He took off his hat and bowed his head for a moment. "Thank you, Spring Maiden," he called. "Bless this house and all those who live here. We remember the ancient symbol of renewing life and hope."

The Spring Maiden smiled, and all the colors of the plants and trees and even the little house seemed brighter to Fluff. The little Sun King waved to the children, and the sun shone warmer and everything seemed to grow a little more.

All day the Spring Maiden and the little Sun King went about the world, leaving the red eggs and spring flowers. They blessed everything and everyone, and Fluff went with them. As the sun began to set and the sky darkened with the coming night, Fluff realized he was very sleepy.

"Dear little rabbit, you have been so wonderful to help us," the Lady said, as she knelt to rub Fluff's ears. "I will take you back to your meadow now, if you wish."

"I would rather stay with you, Lady, and with the Sun King," Fluff answered. "But I am only a small rabbit and really not important,

I know. Even though the children all called me a messenger of the Goddess."

"But you are special, Fluff," said the little Sun King as he gathered the rabbit into his arms. "Don't you know that everything in this world is important to me and to my Mother? And you are very special because you have so much yet to do. I will keep you with me always, Fluff." Fluff snuggled down in the Sun King's arms and yawned. "Some people don't believe in the Goddess or in me anymore. But even though their minds say it is all superstition and nonsense, their hearts and souls will remember the truth. And every spring when they see you, they will remember to celebrate the joy of renewing life and the ancient truth that my Mother and I will always love and care for them."

"Dear little Fluff, come and live with us in the Sacred Grove." The Spring Maiden smiled when Fluff nodded that he would.

The Goddess gave a special blessing to the little rabbit, so he could remain the special friend and companion of Her son, the Sun King. Fluff and the Sun King are born together, grow up together, die at the same time, and are reborn together.

Fluff still lives in the Sacred Grove and each spring he goes through the world with the Spring Maiden and the little Sun King, reminding the people and animals and plants that there is always hope and new life. They carry their gifts of the special colored eggs and spring flowers to all the children. The children still love Fluff and call him the messenger of the Goddess.

The Sacred Wedding
(Beltane—May 1)

"Wake up! Wake up!" cried a group of elves outside the oak-home of the littlest Faeries in the forest. "Wake up, sleepy heads!"

"My goodness, who is shouting?" asked the Faery named Rose, as she sat up and rubbed at her eyes. "It is so early, the Sun isn't awake yet."

"Tell them to go away." Lilac covered her head with the eiderdown blanket as she tried to go back to sleep. "I'm tired."

The elves knocked loudly on the door to the little home under the roots of the great oak tree. "Hurry, Faeries! We must not be late for the wedding."

"Oh my! I forgot about the wedding!" Elder Blossom threw back the blankets and ran to wash her face with spring water that they kept in an acorn shell.

"We're coming!" called out Dandelion as she pulled on her finest dress of woven spider silk and flower petals. She quickly brushed her long golden hair and tied it with a bright red ribbon.

Daffodil, Meadow-Grass, and Lilac hurried to get dressed in their finest clothes, too. The dresses were carefully made out of cobwebs, flowers, bright leaves, and moss. When all the little Faeries were washed and dressed and had brushed their hair, they ran to the door and opened it.

There, the group of tall, beautiful elves waited. Some of them carried harps and bagpipes and flutes. And coming down the path through the forest, they saw Brown Knobby, the gnome, with his fiddle slung over his back.

"Good morning, Faeries," said the elf named Merry. "We thought we should remind you about the Sacred Wedding this day." He smiled down at the little Faeries. "After all, you do not know enough yet to remember the festivals of the forest."

"Thank you," said Rose. She felt very shy beside the tall elves.

"Hello, little Faeries." Brown Knobby was dressed in his best brown clothes. His round, dark eyes twinkled as he greeted them. "You look very nice this morning. The Queen of the May and the Lord of the Greenwood will be happy when they see you."

"What will happen at this wedding?" Elder Blossom asked the gnome, as she hurried along the forest path beside him. "What are we supposed to do?"

"The elfin ladies and other Faeries will tell you what to do," Brown Knobby said. "There will be a wedding and then everyone will dance and celebrate. It will be great fun."

"I've never danced before." Little Meadow-Grass skipped along, her long curls bouncing on her back. "Is dancing hard?"

"No," answered the gnome with a smile. "You just let the music move your feet."

The Faeries and their friends came out of the forest into the meadow. The grass was covered with dewdrops that shone like stars from the first rays of the sun that peeked over the trees. In the center of the meadow was a very tall pole, all hung with lots and lots of colored ribbons. Tables were set up near the trees and covered with all kinds of cakes and good food. Many elves and Faeries and brownies and gnomes were hurrying around, tending to the food and decorating with early May flowers. A brightly colored tent was set up by the far side of the meadow.

"How lovely," Rose said and clapped her hands together.

"Come, little Faeries," said a tall elfin lady who was waiting for them. The lady's dress was a sky blue with lace on the sleeves. "We need your help." She held out a silver chalice to the little Faeries. "The Queen of the May always washes Her face with morning dew. Please fill this cup with dew from the grass in the meadow."

"It's awfully big, isn't it?" said Daffodil, as she, Dandelion, and Elder Blossom carried the silver cup. Meadow-Grass, Lilac, and Rose began to gather the dewdrops from the wet grass and pour them into the cup. "Maybe we are being punished because we stayed in bed so long."

"Maybe we will never get it filled." Meadow-Grass began to cry. Some of her tears fell into the silver cup with the dewdrops.

"We have to try." Rose wiped the tears from her little sister's eyes. "If we work hard and fill the cup, surely they will let us see this wedding."

The little Faeries gathered dewdrops until the silver cup was full to the top. Then they proudly carried it to the elfin lady, who was waiting beside the colorful tent in the shade of the forest trees.

"Thank you," she said. "You are helpful little Faeries. Would you like to come inside and see the Queen?"

"Oh, yes!" they all said.

The lady held aside the tent flap, and the little Faeries tiptoed inside. There, they saw a very beautiful woman sitting on a golden chair. The Maiden was brushing the woman's long hair with a brush made of shells.

"We know the Maiden," whispered Rose.

"So they have come at last." The beautiful woman turned on the chair and looked down at the Faeries. "Thank you, little ones, for gathering the dewdrops for Me."

The woman's eyes were shining with a bright light. Her long dress was green as the tree leaves, and Her slippers were golden as the summer sun. Around Her neck hung necklace of deep green stones. On Her fingers were gold and silver rings. She took the silver cup and gently washed Her face with the dewdrops the Faeries had gathered. When She was finished, a beautiful light shone from Her face.

"Are you the Queen of the May?" Dandelion finally asked in a hushed voice.

The woman smiled. "Yes, at this time of year I am Queen of the May. But look again, little Faeries. Do you know who I am at other times?"

"You are the Goddess." Little Daffodil's eyes were very wide.

"You have learned the secret, I see." The Queen smiled at them. "Today, I wed the Lord of the Greenwood, so that the energies of the Earth and the sun and the sky and the waters will all be strong. When these energies are strong, it means that the plants and animals and all life will be strong. And when all life is strong, then each year there will be new baby plants and animals and birds and all kinds of new little creatures."

The Queen stood up, and the Maiden placed a garland of flowers in Her hair. As the Queen walked toward the door, Lilac shyly stepped forward.

"Goddess, the train of Your dress will get all wet from the dew-covered grass," Lilac said. "Is there no one to carry it for You?"

"Now I wonder who I can get to do that for Me?" The Goddess smiled at the little Faeries. "I wonder if My littlest Faeries would carry the train of my dress?"

"Oh, yes!" the Faeries said.

"Then you shall be part of my wedding." The Goddess waited for the little Faeries to pick up the end of Her dress. Then She walked out into the early morning sun.

Everyone in the forest was waiting outside. Next to the tall pole with the bright ribbons stood the Lord of the Greenwood. He was dressed all in forest green and wore a hat with a long feather in it. Music started as the Goddess slowly walked toward Her Lord.

"There is Brown Knobby, playing his fiddle," whispered Rose. "He is smiling at us."

The little Faeries proudly carried the Queen of the May's dress train through the crowd and right up to the Maypole. They watched happily as the Queen of the May and the Lord of the Greenwood exchanged rings and promised to care for each other and all of the creatures in the world. Just as the Queen and Her Lord kissed, the sun came out over the trees and the dew on the grass in the meadow looked like a thousand sparkling diamonds.

"Now we all shall dance and be happy!" said the Queen of the May. Then She smiled down at the little Faeries. "And thank you for helping Me," She said.

The Lord of the Greenwood took the Queen by the hand, and they danced over the meadow. All around them, the elves and Faeries and gnomes and brownies danced too.

Finally, the Lord and Lady motioned everyone to pick up the end of a ribbon, and everyone danced and danced around the Maypole, weaving colored patterns and laughing.

After the dancing, they all ate a wedding breakfast and danced some more. Just as the little Faeries were getting tired, the Queen of the May approached them.

"Here is a present for each of you," She said, and gave each Faery a flower from the garland in Her hair. "When you use these, you will remember Me." She smiled down at their sleepy faces.

"Oh, look!" Meadow-Grass said as the Queen went off to dance with Her Lord again. The flowers had all turned into little silver combs, just right for combing the Faeries' silky long hair.

The little Faeries curled up under a maple tree, yawned once, and fell asleep to the sound of the magickal fiddles and bagpipes and flutes.

Jason and the Faery Ring

(Summer Solstice—June)

"There aren't such things as Faeries," Jason said, looking down at the face of his little sister. Jason was ten years old and didn't want Julie's talk about Faeries to embarrass him in front of his friends. "Only little kids believe in Faeries."

"There are too Faeries," Julie answered, stamping her foot.

"Aren't." Jason frowned at his six-year-old sister.

"Are!" Julie frowned back and stuck out her tongue.

"Prove it," Jason said. "They don't teach about Faeries in school, so there aren't any."

"Schools don't know everything. Mom and Dad say there are Faeries. There's even a Faery ring in our back yard where they come and dance." Julie started to cry, she was so upset with her brother. "I'll tell the Faeries to take away your model airplane. That will teach you, Jason!" She turned and ran back to the house.

"Little sisters," Jason said to himself as he walked away to find his friends and play baseball.

By the time he came home for supper, he had forgotten all about his argument with Julie and her threat about the Faeries. But when he went into his room to go to bed, his prize model airplane was gone.

"I haven't seen your plane," his mother said when he asked, "and Julie hasn't been in your room. She's played in the backyard all afternoon."

Jason was very upset and unhappy when he went to bed. He lay there a long time, wondering who had taken his plane. He knew his parents didn't allow Julie to come into his room and mess with his things. But if Julie didn't take the plane, who did?

He had a strange feeling that he should look outside, at the backyard. The Moon was full and bright, and its light made it possible for Jason to see as clear as day. He pressed his face closer to the window and looked at the Faery ring. There in the center of the dark green circle of grass sat his model airplane.

"It wasn't there before," he whispered. "And Julie is asleep. So who took my plane and put it outside?"

Jason's bare feet made no noise as he quietly opened the back door and went out into the bright moonlight. He hurried across the lawn and stepped inside the dark ring of grass to pick up his airplane. But when he turned to go back, the house was gone. Little lights like fireflies darted all around him.

"What's happening?" Jason said, and he was afraid.

"You are between the worlds in the land of Faeries," said a voice.

Jason turned and saw a man standing beside him. The man looked different somehow, but Jason couldn't decide why. "Who are you?" he finally asked.

"My name is Fire Glow, and I am a Faery," the man answered. "Hurry now. We must not be late for the Summer Solstice celebration or the Faery Queen will be upset."

"There aren't any Faeries." Jason looked for his house, but he still couldn't see it. "Faeries are make-believe."

"Is that so?" Fire Glow said. He reached out and gave a little pull on Jason's hair.

"Ouch! That hurt." Jason frowned, but Fire Glow grinned at him.

"How can that hurt?" the man asked. "After all, I don't exist. I'm only make-believe."

"Prove you are a Faery," Jason demanded. "Take me to this Faery Queen of yours if you can."

"The magic words," Fire Glow said with a grin, as he put three leaves into the pocket of Jason's pajamas.

"What are these?" Jason asked, as he felt for the leaves.

"Leaves of oak, ash, and hawthorn. They will help you travel to the court of the Faery Queen. And they will help you return home when your visit is over."

Fire Glow took Jason's hand while he sprinkled something over the boy's head. For a moment everything seemed to be spinning, then it stopped, and Jason stood in the middle of a large grassy space with thick trees around the edges.

"We are just in time," Fire Glow said. "Here comes the court and the Queen now."

Out of the trees came a parade of strange beings, some tall, some small, and others very tiny. They were laughing and singing as they came. Some walked, some rode horses, and, when Jason looked very carefully, he saw that the tiny ones rode on little mice.

At the head of this parade rode a beautiful woman on a dappled gray horse. She was dressed in a brightly colored long dress and had flowers in her long hair. The saddle and bridle of her horse were decorated with silver and gold. In one hand she held a silver wand with a crystal on the end. Beside her rode a man with dark hair and a sword by his side.

"I'm dreaming, that's all," Jason said, then jumped as Fire Glow laughed and tugged at his hair again. "It sure seems like it," Jason grumbled, as he smoothed down his hair.

The parade of Faery beings poured into the clearing until they filled the space. Jason forgot to say anything else about dreaming and make-believe, he was so interested in watching these strange creatures. The little darting lights he had seen when first he stepped into the Faery ring once more flew around his head. This time he saw that they were really tiny people with fluttering wings.

The Queen and King dismounted and sat on flower-covered chairs as their attendants led away their horses. All around the clearing, tables were set up with food and drink. Some of the people began to play on pipes and harps, filling the moonlit night with beautiful music.

"Bring the boy Jason to us," called out the Queen. "I would like to talk with this human child who says we do not exist."

Fire Glow took Jason's arm and pulled him forward to stand before the Queen. "I have brought him by the power of oak, ash, and thorn," the Faery man said with a bow.

"Why do you say we are not real?" the King asked, as he leaned forward to look at Jason with dark eyes. "You can see and hear and feel us. Does that not make us real?"

"Well, other kids don't see you," Jason answered. "And I never saw you before."

"Did anyone else see the deer you saw last fall, standing under the trees along the road?" The Queen smiled when Jason shook his head. "So the deer does not exist then?"

"Yes, they exist. Everyone sees deer." Jason was beginning to feel he just might be wrong.

"Everyone?" The King raised his eyebrows in question.

"Well, no, I suppose everyone doesn't see deer," Jason answered. "Deer move very quiet and usually stay away from people. You have to stand very still and be patient to see a deer."

"Have you ever seen a dinosaur or a dodo bird?" The Queen tapped her wand on her knee.

Jason shook his head. "They're all dead now."

"Then they never existed, if you haven't seen one." The King took a goblet offered to him. "They are make-believe."

"I've read books that tell all about them," Jason protested. He stopped and thought. *I've read books about Faeries too. And now I'm seeing them. Maybe I was wrong when I said there are no Faeries.*

"Yes, perhaps you were wrong in thinking that," the Queen said with a smile as she read his thoughts. "Like the deer, we do not show ourselves to just anyone. Like the deer, there are those who would try to destroy us if they could. But Faeries and other such creatures do like to meet and talk with humans who believe in us. We sometimes help these believers and try to teach them ancient knowledge that is not written down in books."

"Let us eat and drink and be merry while the night lasts," the King said.

Jason and Fire Glow sat on the grass by the Queen and King while the musicians played and food was passed around. Jason was surprised to learn that the goblets held flower nectar and that the strange food was made from mushrooms and other natural things.

"Why did you bring me here?" Jason finally asked the Faery Queen. "I was being rude when I said you didn't exist."

"You have a special task ahead of you when you grow up." The Faery King looked down at Jason, his dark eyes intent. "You and many other humans will have the task of making your world a better place to live. Although we seldom live within your world, we are part of it. If your world is destroyed, then so is our world. We are part of each other and must work together."

"At one time, in the distant past," the Queen said softly, "humans and the Faery folk were closer than we are now. We want to make the ties between us stronger, not weaker. Will you help?"

"If I can," Jason answered. "Will I remember you when I go home?" *How can I ever forget the pipers and the dancing and the wonderful food,* he thought, as he glanced around the clearing.

"I will give you something to help you remember us." The King pointed at Jason's pajama pocket. "Take out the leaves and think of your home," he said.

Jason held the three leaves in his hands as he thought of the Faery ring in the grass in his backyard. As everything started to spin around him, he suddenly cried, "Wait!"

But it was too late. He stood in the center of the Faery ring outside his back door. He held his airplane in one hand. The leaves in his other hand crumbled into dust in the moonlight. *The Faery King was going to give me something, but he forgot,* Jason thought, and he was sad.

Just then, something fell onto the grass and glittered in the light of the Moon. Jason picked it up and found that he held a little silver ring in his hand. He smiled as he heard the laughter of the Faery King.

The back door of the house opened, and Jason's mother stood there in her nightgown. "What are you doing?" she asked.

Jason ran to her and told her of his wonderful journey. He showed her the little ring.

"I had forgotten," his mother said softly. "Feasting with the Faeries is so wonderful." She touched a tiny ring she wore on her little finger, then patted Jason's shoulder. "Go back to bed now."

Jason peeked out the window before he went back to his room and saw his mother, her bare feet white in the moonlight, standing in the center of the Faery ring with her arms raised toward the Moon.

"I guess you don't have to be a kid to believe in the Faeries," he said to himself. He went to bed and dreamed of the strange Faery world and the King's gift.

The Grain Mother
(Lammas and Lunasa—August 1)

The summer sun was very bright and hot. It turned the grass in the meadow brown and dry. All the birds and animals huddled in the shade under the trees so they could be cool in the heat of late summer. Deep under the roots of the giant oak in the shady forest a group of little Faeries sat in their home, drinking glasses of cool flower nectar.

"It will soon be time for us to go to the meadow," the Faery named Lilac said, as she fanned herself with a little oak leaf. "It seems as if we have been harvesting food forever."

"The squirrel says winter will soon come, and we will need the food to eat then." Little Meadow-Grass sighed and looked at the baskets of grass seeds, dried mushrooms, acorns, and sweet-smelling flower petals that filled the shelves around all the rooms. "Surely this will be enough food for us."

"What is winter?" asked Rose, as she finished making a hat of leaves and moss to keep off the hot sun. "We have never seen winter."

"The squirrel says winter is very, very cold." Daffodil piled the last of their empty baskets near the door. "He and the birds say the wind blows and first it rains and then it snows."

"I don't think I will like snow." Dandelion put an apron on over her white dress. "I asked the great oak today about snow, and it told me that snow is wetter and colder than anything we have ever seen."

"Then I don't think I will like snow either." Elder Blossom finished weaving her big grass-stem basket and set it aside.

"The Faeries who live under the big maple tree near the pond told me there will be a special celebration tonight when the harvest is finished," Lilac said. "They said the Grain Mother will be there."

All the Faeries looked in surprise at Lilac, who shrugged and shook her head.

"When I asked them who the Grain Mother was, they laughed at me," she said. "I was embarrassed that I didn't know."

"We don't know either," the other little Faeries answered. "Will the others let us go to the celebration if we don't know who the Grain Mother is?"

Lilac shrugged again. "I don't know," she answered.

There was a knock on the tiny door to their underground home.

"Open up, Faeries," called a loud voice. "It's nearly time to go harvesting."

Rose opened the door, and the little gnome Brown Knobby hurried inside. He took off his brown hat and smiled at the little Faeries. The sleeves of his brown shirt were rolled up above his elbows. Several grass-woven bags were thrown over his shoulder. One of the bags held his fiddle.

"Brown Knobby, who is the Grain Mother?" Daffodil asked, as she poured the gnome a glass of flower nectar.

"The Grain Mother is just another face of the Great Mother," the gnome answered, as he looked at the Faeries with round dark eyes. "When the Mother appears as the Grain Mother, the humans sometimes called Her Demeter or Ceres. She blesses the grain and all the food that is harvested for the winter." His eyes twinkled. "Maybe I shouldn't let you go to the celebration if you don't know about the Grain Mother."

"Don't tease us, Brown Knobby!" Little Dandelion looked as if she were going to cry. "We're only new little Faeries. We are still learning, you know."

The gnome smiled and bowed to the Faeries. "You can come with me," he said, his dark eyes twinkling. "I will introduce you to the Grain Mother when She comes to the harvest festival." He smiled even more, and then said, "The Sun King will be there, too."

The little Faeries gathered up their baskets and bags and a picnic lunch. Then they all hurried out toward the meadow with Brown Knobby. Other Faeries, gnomes, elves, and brownies were already filling their pouches and bags with the last of the grass seeds.

"Look! There is the Queen of the Faeries, and the King!" Rose pointed across the meadow. A regal looking woman, with her long hair braided back, was helping with the harvesting. Beside her worked a handsome man with dark hair, his sleeves rolled up like Brown Knobby's.

"Everyone helps at the harvest," the gnome said. "Everyone must help to gather food for winter."

The gnome and the Faeries began to fill their baskets with grass seeds. They gathered the fallen acorns and the mushrooms that grew at the edges of the forest. Finally, the sun went down, and a big, round moon came sliding up the sky.

"It's cooler now," said Elder Blossom, as they stacked all their filled baskets and bags together. "Look at the moon. Isn't she beautiful tonight?"

The gnome and the Faeries went to the edge of a little stream and washed their hands and faces. Brown Knobby brought out the big picnic basket and a jug of apple cider. Rose and Dandelion spread a blanket on the grass near a tree, and they all sat down to eat. All around them, other little Faeries and elves and gnomes and brownies were resting and eating too.

"Listen!" said Brown Knobby. "She is coming! The Grain Mother is coming!"

The little Faeries listened. Everyone in the meadow was quiet. Lilac saw several deer silently step out of the trees and wait along the edge of the meadow. A white owl settled on a limb above their heads, and a pair of squirrels dashed down a tree trunk to sit beside the Faeries.

"I don't hear anything," Lilac said, looking around.

"Listen to the breeze," answered the gnome. "You can hear the footsteps of the Grain Mother."

The Faeries listened very carefully and heard the sound of some-one walking through dry grass. Swish, swish, went the sound. They watched as the Faery King and Queen stood up and faced the far end of the meadow.

A tall woman stepped out of the forest and walked out into the meadow. She wore a gold and green dress. Her bright yellow hair was braided around Her head, and She was smiling.

"Is that the Grain Mother?" Elder Blossom's little mouth made an O of delight, as she looked at the beautiful lady. "Oh, look! The Sun King is coming along behind Her, and His arms are full of ripe grapes and fruit."

"And there is the Maiden and the Old Wise One." Rose clasped her hands together in joy. "Oh, it's so wonderful, Brown Knobby! And listen, even the trees and wind are singing to Her."

The Faeries all looked up at the great trees of the forest and heard the wind whispering through the branches. The rustle of the leaves and movement of the tree limbs made a special song. The white owl hooted once, spread its mighty wings, and flew to meet the Grain Mother. The golden-haired Mother raised her arm, and the owl settled gently on it.

"Greetings, my children." The Grain Mother's voice carried like music on the little night breeze. "I am so glad you remembered to come and celebrate the harvest with Me."

Everyone around the meadow bowed to the Lady as She walked along, blessing each of them. When She came to the little Faeries, She stopped and touched each one of them on the head with Her hand.

"Welcome, little ones. I am so happy to see new little children at My festivals. Are you all happy?"

"Yes, Lady," they all said together, as they looked up into Her beautiful eyes.

The Grain Mother moved on to a fallen tree, where the Maiden spread a green cloak for Her to sit upon.

"Her eyes were blue as the hot summer sky," Lilac said.

"Yes, but they were also the blue of the secret, shady forest pond, where the turtles and fish live," Rose answered.

The little Faeries watched in fascination as the Sun King squeezed the juice from the grapes and fruit into a big cauldron that the Old Wise One set near the Grain Mother.

"Now we will all have even more fun," said Brown Knobby as he took his fiddle out of one of his bags and began to tune it. "Tonight we will dance in honor of the Lady and the Sun King."

Other fiddles and bagpipes and flutes sounded all around the clearing, making beautiful music. The Grain Mother clapped Her hands to the music. Soon everyone there, even the new little Faeries, were dancing and laughing to the music. The Sun King and the Grain Mother danced together, while the Old Wise One took a ladle and filled all the cups and glasses with the juice. Little clouds of fireflies glowed around the dancers.

Later, the Maiden came to Brown Knobby and made him put down his fiddle to dance with Her. Brown Knobby's cheeks turned pink with surprise and happiness. He bowed to the Maiden, and they whirled out onto the meadow in a spinning dance.

"Now I see," said Dandelion, when she and her sisters stopped dancing for a while to rest. "Harvest isn't all work. It is also a celebration that we have food for the coming cold times. It is all very wonderful."

The Faeries watched the dancers and the fireflies for a time, before they fell asleep on the blankets, tired and happy. When Brown Knobby woke them to take them home, he was humming a dance tune. And he hummed it all the way back to the great oak and the Faeries' little home.

The Maiden's Journey
(Autumn Equinox—September)

It was autumn in the great forest. All the leaves were gold and red and brown. Some of the leaves had fallen to the ground, where they lay in colorful piles around the huge trees. The squirrels were busy in the pine and fir trees, gathering and hiding the nuts from the tree cones.

The littlest Faeries in the forest were busy too. They already had their winter supply of food tucked away in their home under the roots of the great oak tree. Now they were gathering bits of moss and long strings of cobwebs, discarded feathers and pieces of fur the animals had left on the bushes. They would use these for weaving dresses and capes and hats and blankets during the cold winter days ahead.

The little Faery Daffodil stopped winding the cobwebs on her stick and stood very still. "Listen," she said. "Someone is walking through the forest."

"Should we hide?" Meadow-Grass looked afraid.

"No, I don't think so," answered her sister Rose. "Humans don't usually see us, and the animals don't harm us."

The six Faeries waited and watched as the sound of steps got closer. Then, along the faint path came the beautiful young Maiden. She was dressed all in white and Her hair was braided down her back. She was wearing a dark blue cape that reminded the Faeries of the night sky.

"Good morning, Faeries," the Maiden said as She stopped to look at them.

"Good morning, Maiden," the Faeries answered. "Where are you going?"

"I'm going on a journey," the Maiden said.

"May we walk with You?" Little Elder Blossom asked shyly.

"It is a long journey." The Maiden smiled down at her. "I will be gone until Winter Solstice. But you may walk with me part of the way. I would be glad to have your company."

The Faeries stacked all their material near a root of a big fir tree and walked along with the Maiden. They went deeper and deeper into the forest, where the shadows were thick and heavy underneath the tall trees. The path the Maiden took finally went up a forest-covered hill and ended at the dark opening of a cave.

The little Faeries stopped and stared at the cave.

"Are you going inside?" asked Lilac. She shivered because she was very afraid.

"Yes, I must go inside." The Maiden sat down on a big rock, and the Faeries gathered around Her. "The path goes through the cave. Then it goes down and down into the Earth until it enters the realm of the Dark Lord. I must go into the Dark Lord's realm and stay until the Winter Solstice. Then I will come back for a time and celebrate with you."

"Oh, no!" Dandelion started to cry. "You mustn't go there! You might get lost and we would never see You again."

The Maiden picked up Dandelion and wiped away the Faery's tears. "I go every year," She said. "I know the path very well and will not get lost. You must not be afraid for Me, little ones. It is very important that I go."

"But why?" Meadow-Grass looked up at the Maiden with sad eyes. "What could be more important than the forest and all who live here?"

"Go ask the Old Wise One in the Sacred Grove, little Faeries," said a deep voice from the cave. "Come, my Lady. They are waiting."

The Faeries turned to see a tall dark man wearing a fur cloak and carrying a spear. He stood just inside the cave with the dark shadows close about him. He held out His hand to the Maiden, and She disappeared into the cave with Him.

"Come back!" cried all the Faeries. "Maiden, come back!"

But the Maiden was gone, and they were alone on the hill.

"We must tell the Mother!" Rose began to run down the hill, and her little sisters ran with her.

The Faeries ran and ran until they were very tired.

"Where are you going in such a hurry?" croaked a big raven, who watched them from a tree limb.

"We must find the Mother," said Lilac. "We must tell Her that the Dark Lord took the Maiden down into His realm."

The raven cawed loudly, then flew down to the ground beside the Faeries. Other ravens also flew down to sit beside them.

"Climb on our backs," the first raven said. "We will take you to the Sacred Grove. But you mustn't be afraid, little Faeries. The Maiden goes every year into the Dark Lord's realm."

"But why?" asked Dandelion as they climbed on the birds' backs. "I don't understand."

"The Old Wise One will explain it to you," said the raven. Then the ravens all flew away through the forest.

"Oh, the ground is far away," said Daffodil, peeking through her fingers she had over her eyes.

"But it is fun," answered Rose. "You can see so far from up here. Look! There is the Sacred Grove and all the big stones that guard it."

She pointed ahead. The Faeries could see the big gray stones and the open space in the center with the altar stone.

"The Old Wise One is waiting there for us," Dandelion said, and pointed to an old woman in a black dress who sat on the altar stone.

The ravens flew down to light beside the Old Wise One. The little Faeries climbed down to the ground. All the ravens flew away, except the biggest one.

"Lady, these little ones do not know why the Maiden went on Her journey," cawed the big raven. The bird nodded its head to the old woman, and She nodded back. "They are afraid they will never see Her again."

"Thank you for bringing them to Me." The Old Wise One gathered the Faeries in Her hands and lifted them to the altar stone beside Her. "Now tell Me," she said, "why are you afraid?"

"The cave is very dark and cold." Elder Blossom shivered.

"The Dark Lord looks very frightening." Daffodil hung onto Lilac's hand.

"The Maiden will be gone a long, long time, and we will miss Her." Dandelion looked as if she were going to cry again.

"What do you think lies in the cave at the end of the path?" The Old Wise One smiled at them. "The night is dark, and you are not afraid of the night, are you?"

The Faeries shook their heads.

"Sometimes it is cold when it rains. You are not afraid of rain, are you?"

"No," the Faeries answered. "But what is at the end of the path inside the cave?"

The Old Wise One took the little Faeries into Her lap. "The Dark Lord rules over the land where all creatures go when they die," She said. "It is a place where the souls all sleep and grow strong before they are reborn into a new life."

"But why does the Maiden go there?" asked Meadow-Grass.

"The Maiden goes to comfort them," answered the Old Wise One. "She helps them prepare to return in another body. When it is time for some creature to die, the Dark Lord helps them find their way into His realm. He does this because he follows My laws. He is My helper. The Maiden also follows My laws and goes to help the souls in the Dark Lord's realm."

"We will miss the Maiden." Rose looked up at the Old Wise One and saw the love in Her eyes and in Her smile. "Everywhere She went, the forest was happy."

"The Maiden must go for another reason too." The Old Wise One stroked Daffodil's long silky hair with one wrinkled finger. "When the Maiden awakes from Her long sleep, it is spring in the world. She dances through the summer and into the autumn. Now She must go about Her business, and while She is gone, winter comes. And winter comes so all the plants and animals can rest and prepare for the spring again."

"Then the Maiden is safe?" Elder Blossom snuggled close to the Wise Old One.

"Yes, the Maiden is very safe. No harm shall come to Her."

The Faeries sat in the Old Wise One's lap while She sang them songs about the turn of the seasons and about being reborn. The raven nodded along with the words and waited patiently until the Old Wise One finished Her songs.

"Now, little Faeries, it is time for you to go home," the raven said as the Old Wise One gently lifted them back to the ground. He cawed loudly, and all the other ravens returned to sit beside him. "It will soon be night, and little Faeries need their sleep. We will stop and get your cobwebs and things at the big fir tree. Then we will take you to your home under the oak."

The Faeries climbed back on the ravens. "Goodbye," they called to the Old Wise One.

"Goodbye," She called to them. "Come back at Winter Solstice to the Grove."

"We will," promised the Faeries, and the ravens flew away into the forest.

The Faeries got all the things they'd left at the fir tree. Then the ravens took them right to their door. They thanked the birds for their help and went inside.

"I will still feel sad about the Maiden," Daffodil said, as she put away her sticks wound full of cobwebs.

"I think the secret is that it's all right to miss someone who is gone," said Lilac. "But we should remember that they will always come back. The Dark Lord's realm and winter are not the end of life."

"Then we should plan a surprise for the Maiden." Little Meadow-Grass smiled, as she carefully laid the moss and feathers and bits of fur on a shelf.

"When She returns, we can make Her a garland of spring flowers," said Elder Blossom.

"And we can brush Her long hair and braid it with strands of sweet-smelling herbs." Rose and Dandelion began to dance around the room, they were so happy with their plans.

The little Faeries ate their supper of berries and grass seeds. And for dessert they had candied buttercups and spiced mushrooms. Then they climbed into their little beds and dreamed of all the nice things they wanted to do when the Maiden returned in the spring.

The Troll Tear

(Halloween or Samhain—October 31)

The night was very dark with a Full Moon hanging in the cloud-filled sky above. The air was crisp with the feel of late autumn and the doorway between the worlds was wide open. Carved pumpkins sat on the porches of houses in the little town, and the laughter of children dressed in costumes could be heard from the streets as they paraded from house to house.

But it was a sad time for Beth as she climbed the little hill behind her house. In her arms was her cat and friend Smoky, carefully wrapped in his favorite blanket. A little grave was already dug on the hill, waiting, for Smoky had died that day.

"Do you want me to go with you?" Beth's father had asked. "I dug his grave beside MacDougal's at the top of the hill."

Beth clearly remembered when their dog MacDougal had died after being hit by a car when she was younger. "No, I want to go by myself," she answered.

Beth stopped at the top of the hill and knelt beside the little grave. She carefully laid Smoky's blanket-wrapped form in the earth and covered it with dirt, on the top laying several large rocks. Then she cried and cried.

"Oh, Smoky, I miss you so much!" Beth looked up at the Moon, tears streaming down her cheeks. "Why did you have to die?"

"It was his time to rejoin the Mother," said a deep, gentle voice in the darkness.

"Who said that?" Beth looked around in the dark but saw no one.

"Dying is part of the cycle of life, you know." One of the boulders on the hill stirred into life, and a strange little woman stood up.

"Who are you?" The moonlight shone down on the little woman, and Beth could see it was not a human who stood there.

"I'm a troll-wife," said the creature, as she came to sit across from Beth. "This is a sad night for both of us, Girl. I, too, came to this hill to bury a friend." The troll-wife wiped away a crystal tear from her cheek. "The squirrel was very old. His time was ended. Still, it makes me sad."

Beth stared at the troll-wife. The little woman was the color of rock in the moonlight, her hair like long strands of dried moss, her bright eyes like shining crystals. Her nose was like a little pebble in the center of her face. She wore a dress woven of oak leaves and tree bark. The raven feathers in her dark cloak glistened in the moonlight.

"The squirrel and I lived together for a long time," the troll-wife said. "Like you and Smoky. We often talked to your cat when he was hunting here on the hill. Smoky and I were friends. I shall miss him too." The little woman patted Smoky's grave with a gentle hand. "Sleep well, little friend. When you are rested, we shall talk together again."

"But he's dead," Beth said, her voice choked with tears. "No one can talk to Smoky again."

"Child, this is Samhain. Don't you know the ancient secrets of this sacred time of year?" The troll-wife motioned for Beth to come and sit beside her. "It is true that our friends have gone into a world where we can no longer physically touch them, but the Great Mother has given us other ways of communicating with them. We can do this any time, but the time of Samhain is the easiest."

Beth was not afraid when the troll-wife put her arm around her shoulders. The troll-wife's skin was rough and as warm as a rock heated by the Sun.

"I don't understand how this can be done," Beth said, "or why Samhain makes it easier."

"At this time of year," the troll-wife answered, "the walls between this world and the world of spirits and souls are very thin. If we are quiet and listen, we can hear our loved ones and they can hear us. We talk, not in spoken words, by with the heart and mind."

"Isn't that just imagination?" Beth looked down at Smoky's grave, tears once more coming into her eyes. "Like my thinking I can feel MacDougal get up on my bed at night like he used to do?"

"Sometimes it is, but mostly it is not imagination, but our friends come to see us in their spirit bodies." The troll-wife reached out her hand and patted something on her shoulder that Beth couldn't see. "Like my friend the Raven. He is here now."

Beth looked hard and saw a thin form of hazy moonlight on the troll-wife's shoulder. "I've seen something like that at the foot of my bed where MacDougal used to sleep," she whispered. "I thought I was dreaming." She jumped as something nudged her arm. When she looked down, nothing was there.

The troll-wife smiled. "Close your eyes and think of MacDougal," she said. "He has been waiting a long time for you to see him."

Beth closed her eyes and, at once, the form of her little dog came into her mind. His tail wagged with happiness as he grinned at her with his silly, little dog-smile. She felt a wave of love come from him, and she sent her love for him back. Then she felt the dog lie down against her leg.

"Can I do this with Smoky?" Beth asked, opening her eyes and looking at the little woman.

"Not yet," the troll-wife answered. "He needs to sleep a while and rest. Then he will come to you. This gives Smoky time to adjust to his new world and you time to grieve for him. It is not wrong to grieve," the woman said. "But we must not grieve forever. We must learn to be happy that our friends have had a birthday in a new world."

"I never thought of it that way," Beth said. "It's kind of like they moved far away, and we can only talk to them on the telephone."

"It is this way with all creatures, not just animals." The troll-wife stood up and held out a hand to Beth. "Will you join me, human girl? Although I have buried my friend squirrel this night, I still must dance and sing to all my friends and ancestors who have gone on their journey into the Otherworld. For this is a time to honor the ancestors and remember all those who have gone before us."

Beth joined the troll-wife in the ancient, slow troll dances around the top of the little hill in the moonlight. She watched quietly while the troll-wife called out troll-words to the four directions, words Beth couldn't understand. But deep in her heart, the girl felt the power of the strange words and knew they were given in honor and love by the little troll-wife.

When the troll-wife finished with her ritual, she hugged Beth. "Go in peace, human child," she said. "And remember what I have told you about the ancient secret of Samhain."

"I will," Beth answered. "Will I ever see you again?"

"Whenever the Moon is full, I will be here," the little troll-wife said. "And especially at Samhain."

"I wish I had something to give you." Beth hugged the little woman. "You have taught me so much." She felt the tears come to her eyes again.

"Let us exchange tears for our lost friends." The troll-wife reached out a rough finger and caught a tear as it fell from Beth's eye. The tear glistened on her finger. The troll-wife gently touched her finger to her cloak, and Beth's tear shone there like a diamond in the moonlight.

Beth reached up carefully and caught one of the troll-wife's tears as it slid down the rough cheek. It turned into a crystal in her hands.

"Remember the secret of Samhain, and remember me," the troll-wife said softly, as she disappeared into the darkness.

Beth walked back down the hill, the crystal clutched in her hand. Her father was waiting for her on the porch.

"Are you all right?" her father asked as he gave Beth a hug.

"I will be," she answered. She opened her hand under the porch light and saw a perfect tear-shaped crystal lying there.

"Did you find something?" her father asked, looking at the crystal.

"A troll-tear," Beth answered, and her father smiled. For he also knew the little troll-wife and the secret of Samhain.

The Yule Faeries
(Winter Solstice—December)

A group of little Faeries huddled in their home deep under the roots of a giant oak tree. They were safe and snug in their tiny underground cave lined with dandelion fluff, bird feathers, and dried moss. Outside, the wind blew cold and the snow fell softly down to cover the ground.

"I saw the Sun King today," the Faery named Rose said, as she pulled her mossy cloak tighter about her. "He looked so old and tired as he walked off through the forest. What is wrong with him?"

"The great oak says he's dying," answered Daffodil.

"Dying? Oh, what will we do now?" Little Meadow-Grass started to cry. "If the Sun King dies, our little plant-friends will not grow. The birds will not come and sing again. Everything will be winter forever!"

Lilac, Dandelion, and Elder Blossom tried to comfort their friend, but they were all very sad. As they huddled together, there was a knock on the tiny door.

"Open up, Faeries," called out a loud voice. "Why are you hiding instead of joining us in our Solstice celebration?"

Rose opened the door, and the little gnome Brown Knobby pushed inside, shaking the glistening snowflakes off his brown coat and hat.

"We are too sad to celebrate," Daffodil said, wiping her eyes. "The Sun King is dying. Haven't you heard?"

"He's dead, you silly Faeries." Brown Knobby's round, dark eyes sparkled with laughter. "Now hurry, or we'll be late for the celebration."

"How can you be happy and laughing?" Elder Blossom stamped her little foot and frowned at the gnome. "If the Sun Kind is dead, it will be winter always. We will never see the Sun again!"

"Silly little child-Faeries." Brown Knobby grabbed Dandelion by the hand and pulled her to her feet. "There is a secret to the Winter Solstice. Don't you want to know what it is?"

The Faeries looked at him in surprise. "Secret?" they all said. "What secret? We are only new little Faeries, you silly gnome. We've never been to a Winter Solstice celebration before."

"Come and see. Come and see. Get your capes and come with me." Brown Knobby danced and jigged around the room. "Hurry, hurry, don't be slow! To the sacred oak grove through the snow!" He danced out the door and disappeared.

"What did that gnome mean?" Rose asked as she gathered up her cloak of dried rose petals held together with cobwebs and lined with goose down.

"I don't know, but the Lady lives in the sacred grove." Meadow-Grass pulled on her hat. "Perhaps if we go to see the Goddess, She can explain what Brown Knobby was talking about."

The Faeries left their snug little home and trudged off through the snow toward the sacred oak grove. The forest was dark with only the light of the Moon shining down through the thick fir branches and bare limbs of maple and hawthorn. It was very difficult for them to get through the snow because they were very, very small. As they waded through the wet snow and shivered in the cold wind, they met a fox.

"Where are you going, Faeries?" the fox asked.

"To the sacred grove," they answered. They were cold and shivering.

"Climb on my back, and I will take you there swiftly." The fox knelt down so the Faeries could climb up on his back. Then he raced off through the dark.

"Listen!" Lilac said, as they neared the grove of sacred trees. "Someone is singing happy songs. A lot of someones."

The beautiful music carried over the cold, still, moonlit air. It was the most beautiful music the Faeries had ever heard. The fox carried the Faeries right to the edge of the stone altar in the center of the grove, and knelt down.

"Look!" said Elder Blossom, as they slid to the snow-covered ground. "There is the Maiden and the Mother and the Old Wise One. And many other of the Small Folk."

"They are all smiling and happy," Lilac said, as she looked around at all the creatures.

"All the animals are too," whispered Dandelion. "Why are they all looking at the Mother?"

The Faeries moved closer to the three Ladies seated on the stone altar. The Mother held a bundle close in Her arms, smiling down at it. The Maiden reached down and took the Faeries gently in Her hands. She held them close to the Mother so they could see what She held.

"A baby!" the Faeries cried. "A new little baby! Look how he glows!"

"He is the newborn Sun King," said the Maiden, smiling.

"But Brown Knobby and the old oak tree said the Sun King was dead," the Faeries answered Her. "How can this little baby be the Sun King?"

"That is the secret of the Winter Solstice." The Wise Old One gently touched the baby's cheek with Her wrinkled hand. "Every year, the old Sun King must come to the sacred grove during the darkest days of winter where he dies. I take his spirit to the Mother who gives him new life again. This is the way of all creatures, not just the Sun King."

"You mean everything lives and dies and lives again?" The Faeries looked down in wonder at the baby Sun King, nestled in the arms of the Mother.

"Yes, little ones," answered the Old Wise One. "There is never an end to life. This is the great mystical secret of the Winter Solstice."

The Faeries laughed because they were so happy.

"I think the little Sun King should have gifts," said Rose. "I will show him where the wild roses bloom in the early summer."

"And I will teach him to call the birds and listen to the songs of the wind," exclaimed Dandelion.

"When he is older and stronger," said the Mother. "Then the flowers will bloom at his touch, the birds will return to sing their songs, the air will be warm from his breath, and winter will be gone for a time. Then the Sun King will run and play with you in the forest."

The little Faeries sang to the baby Sun King their songs of the coming spring, the sweet-smelling flowers, the bumbling bees, and all the secrets of the forest. And all the creatures within the sacred grove sang with them.

Then the fox took them back to their snug home under the roots of the giant oak tree, where they dreamed wonderful dreams of waiting for the warmth of spring and the fun they would have with the little Sun King.

Recommended Reading

Arrowsmith, Nancy, and George Moorse. *A Field Guide to the Little People*. New York: Pocket Books, 1977.

Berk, Ari. *The Runes of Elfland*. New York: Harry N. Abrams, 2003.

Bord, Janet. *Fairies: Real Encounters with Little People*. United Kingdom: Michael O'Mara Books Ltd., 1997.

Briggs, Katharine. *An Encyclopedia of Fairies, Hobgoblins, Brownies, Bogies and Other Supernatural Creatures*. New York: Pantheon Books, 1976.

_____. *The Fairies in Tradition and Literature*. United Kingdom: Routledge & Kegan Paul, 1967.

_____. *The Vanishing People: Fairy Lore & Legends*. New York: Pantheon Books, 1978.

Coghlan, Ronan. *Handbook of Fairies*. United Kingdom: Capall Bann Publishing, 1999.

Colum, Padraic, ed. *A Treasury of Irish Folklore*. New York: Wings Books, 1992.

Conway, D. J. *Advanced Celtic Shamanism*. Freedom, Calif.: The Crossing Press, 2000.

_____. *Celtic Magic*. St. Paul, Minn.: Lewellyn Publications, 1990.

_____. *Magickal, Mythical, Mystical Beasts*. St. Paul, Minn.: Lewellyn Publications, 1996.

Crossley-Holland, Kevin, ed. *Folk Tales of the British Isles*. New York: Pantheon Books, 1985.

Curran, Bob. *A Field Guide to Irish Fairies*. San Francisco, Calif.: Chronicle Books, 1998.

Devereux, Paul. *Fairy Paths & Spirit Roads*. United Kingdom: Vega, 2003.

Dubois, Pierre. *The Great Encyclopedia of Faeries*. New York: Simon & Schuster, Inc., 1996.

Dugan, Ellen. *Garden Witchery*. St. Paul, Minn.: Llewellyn Publications, 2003.

Edwards, Gillian. *Hobgoblin and Sweet Puck*. United Kingdom: Bles, 1974.

Ellis, Peter Berresford. *Dictionary of Celtic Mythology*. United Kingdom: Oxford University Press, 1992.

Evans-Wentz, W. Y. *The Fairy Faith in Celtic Countries*. Secaucus, N.J.: Citadel Press, 1990 (originally published 1911).

Franklin, Anna. *The Illustrated Encyclopedia of Fairies*. United Kingdom: Vega, 2002.

Froud, Brian. *Good Faeries/Bad Faeries*. New York: Simon & Schuster, Inc., 1998.

_____ and Terry Jones. *Lady Cottington's Fairy Album*. New York: Harry N. Abrams, 2002.

Gerard, John. *The Herbal or General History of Plants*. New York: Dover Publications, 1975 (originally published in 1633).

Grieve, M. A. *A Modern Herbal*. New York: Dover Publications, 1982.

Grunwald, Henry Anatole, ed. *The Enchanted World of Fairies and Elves*. Alexandria, Va.: Time-Life, 1984.

Hall, Manly P. *The Secret Teachings of All Ages*. Los Angeles: Philosophical Research Library, 1977.

Hazlett, W. Carew. *Faiths and Folklore of the British Isles*, two volumes. New York: Benjamin Blom, 1965.

Hodson, Geoffrey. *Fairies at Work and Play*. Wheaton, Ill.: Theosophical Publishing House, 1982.

Huygen, Wil. *The Complete Gnomes*. New York: Harry N. Abrams, 1994.

Kane, Tracy. *Fairy Houses*. Lee, N.H.: Light-Beams Publishing, 2001.

Keightley, Thomas. *The World Guide to Gnomes, Fairies, Elves, and Other Little People*. 1880. Reprint, New York: Avenel Books, 1978.

Kirk, Robert. *The Secret Commonwealth*. Edited by Stewart Sanderson. United Kingdom: D. S. Brewer, 1976.

Mack, Carol and Dinah. *A Field Guide to Demons, Fairies, Fallen Angels, and Other Subversive Spirits*. New York: Henry Holt and Co., 1998.

MacKillop, James. *Dictionary of Celtic Mythology*. New York: Oxford University Press, 1998.

MacManus, Diarmaid. *Irish Earth Folk*. New York: Devin-Adair, 1959.

Mager, Marcia Zina. *Believing in Faeries*. United Kingdom: The C. W. Daniel Company Ltd., 1999.

Mann, N. R. *The Celtic Power Symbols*. United Kingdom: Triskele, 1987.

Matthews, John. *Classic Celtic Fairy Tales*. United Kingdom: Blandford, 1997.

McAnally, D. R. *Irish Wonders*. New York: Gramercy Books, 1996.

McCann, Michelle, and Marianne Monson-Burton. *Finding Fairies: Secrets for Attracting Little People From Around the World.* North Vancouver, B.C.: Whitecap Books, 2001.

McCoy, Edain. *A Witch's Guide to Faery Folk.* St. Paul, Minn.: Llewellyn Publications, 1994.

Melville, Francis. *The Book of Faeries.* United Kingdom: Quarto Publishing, 2002.

Mills, Lauren, retold by. *The Book of Little Folk.* New York: Dial Books, 1997.

Nahmad, Claire. *Fairy Spells.* United Kingdom: Souvenir Press, 1997.

O'Rush, Claire. *The Enchanted Garden.* United Kingdom: Trafalgar Square Publishing, 1996.

Parry-Jones, D. *Welsh Legends and Fairy Lore.* New York: Barnes & Noble, 1992.

Patch, H. R. *The Other World.* Cambridge, Mass.: Harvard University Press, 1950.

Penwyche, Gossamer. *The World of Fairies.* New York: Sterling Publishing, 2001.

Riché, David, ed. *The Art of Faery.* United Kingdom: Paper Tiger, 2003.

Robertson, R. MacDonald. *Selected Highland Folktales.* United Kingdom: David & Charles, 1977.

Rose, Carol. *Spirits, Fairies, Leprechauns and Goblins: An Encyclopedia.* New York: W. W. Norton Co., Inc., 1998.

Scalora, Suza. *The Fairies.* New York: Joanna Cotler Books, 1999.

Schwartz, Marla Schram. *Fairy Fun.* New York: Clarkson Potter Publishers, 1998.

Simak, Rudolf. *Dictionary of Northern Mythology.* Translated by Angela Hall. United Kingdom: D. S. Brewer, 1993.

Skene, W. F., trans. *The Four Ancient Books of Wales.* 2 vols. New York: AMS Press, 1984–1985.

Spann, David B. *The Otherworld in Early Irish Literature.* Mich.: University of Michigan, 1969.

Spence, Lewis. *British Fairy Origins.* United Kingdom: Watts, 1946.

————. *The Fairy Traditions in Britain.* United Kingdom: Rider, 1948.

Stanek, Robert. *The Kingdoms & the Elves of the Reaches.* Olympia, Wash.: Virtual Press, 2002.

Stephens, James. *Traditional Irish Fairy Tales.* 1920. Reprint, Mineola, N.Y.: Dover Publications, 1996.

Stewart, R. J. *Robert Kirk: Walker Between Worlds.* United Kingdom: Element Books, 1990.

Tolkien, J.R.R. *The Fellowship of the Ring; The Two Towers;* and *The Return of the King.* Boston, Mass.: Houghton Mifflin Co., 1965.

Van Gelder, Dora. *The Real World of Fairies.* Wheaton, Ill.: Theosophical Publishing House, 1999.

Virtue, Doreen. *Healing With the Fairies.* Carlsbad, Calif.: Hay House, 2001.

Wilde, Lady. *Irish Cures, Mystic Charms and Superstitions.* New York: Sterling Publishing, 1991.

Williams, Rose, retold by. *The Book of Fairies: Nature Spirits From Around the World.* Hillsboro, Ore.: Beyond Words Publishing, 1997.

Yeats, W. B., and Lady Isabella Augusta Gregory. *A Treasure of Irish Myth, Legend & Folklore.* 1888. Reprint, New York: Avenel Books, 1986.

Yolen, Jane, ed. *Favorite Folktales from Around the World.* New York: Pantheon Books, 1986.

Oracle and Tarot Decks

Franklin, Anna. The Fairy Ring. St. Paul, Minn.: Llewellyn Publishing, 2002.

Macbeth, Jessica. The Faeries' Oracle. Illustrated by Brian Froud. New York: Fireside Books, 2000.

Kemp, Gillian. Faerie Wisdom. New York: Sterling Publishing, 2003.

Lupatelli, Antonio. The Fairy Tarots. Italy: Lo Scarabeo, 1998.

Minettei, Riccardo. The Fey Tarot. Italy: Lo Scarabeo, 2002.

Moran, Jaya. Irish Fairy Cards For Inspiration & Guidance. San Antonio, Texas: Word of Wizdom International, 1997.

Virtue, Doreen. Healing With the Fairies. Carlsbad, Calif.: Hay House, 2001.

Wulfing, Sulamith. Fairy Oracle. Amsterdam: S. Wulfing, 1999.

Index

A

adults
  belief in faeries, 7
  contact with faeries, 11
  faery doorways and,
    40, 42
  Law of Power and, 80
aires, 26
Air Faeries, 99–100
anger, spell to dispel,
  106–107
animals, 93
archway, 156
arrow, 157
ash, 163
Asia, Small Folk of, 74–76
auras, 41
Australia, 23, 144
autumn equinox
  faery appearances at, xii
  greeting to faeries, 31
  "The Maiden's Journey"
    story, 196–201
awe, 42–43

B

ballybogs, 129
barbegazi, 128–129
bards, 61
Bassarids, 139
bay laurel, 161
Beauty, Law of, 80–81
befriending. *See* faeries,
  befriending
belief
  in faeries, 7
  for finding faeries, 11

"Jason and the Faery
  Ring" story, 185–191
bells, 19–20
Beltane (May 1)
  appearance of faeries
    on, xii
  greeting to faeries, 31
  "The Sacred Wedding"
    story, 180–185
Bermuda, faeries of, 25–26
Beth, 201–205
birch, 163
bird cage, 168
birdhouse, 168
black dwarves, 136
black feather, 156
blacksmithing
  by dwarves, 135, 136
  Fay craft of, 59–60
  by trolls, 151
Blessed Court. *See* Seelie
  Court
blockages, 84
bluebells, 161
boat, 157
bodies, faery, 1
body, 42–43
boggarts, 130
bogies, 129–130
bokwus, 130
Bonita Maidens, 23
bonsai, 163
borrowing
  by Small Folk, 74, 78–79
  spell to recover borrowed
    objects, 87–89
brain, 42–43
breath
  Air Faeries represent,
    99–100

faery, 78, 79
brown dwarves, 136
brownies
  attachment to
    family, 117
  befriending, 22
  description of, 131–132
Brown Men, 143
Brown Nobby
  in "The Grain Mother"
    story, 192, 193,
    194, 195
  in "The Sacred Wedding"
    story, 181–182, 184
  in "The Yule Faeries"
    story, 205–206, 207
bwbachod (Welsh
  brownie), 131

C

Calvacades. *See* Faery Rides
candle
  Fire Faeries and, 106
  in House Faery
    ritual, 120
  in prosperity spell, 108
  in spell to dispel anger,
    106, 107
  in three wishes ritual,
    114, 115
Carterhaugh, 55
castle, 75
chant
  to Air Faeries, 100
  calling magick from faery
    summer moon ritual,
    47–48
  call within faery circle,
    33–34

(chant, *continued*)
to Desert Faeries, 114
to Earth Faeries, 94
for faery house welcom-
ing ritual, 171
for Faery Land gate, 46
for faery ointment, 97
for Faery oracle, 156
to Fay, 69
to Fire Faeries, 106
greeting to faeries, 31–32
with holey stone, 34–35
in House Faery
ritual, 120
offering stone, 95
in prosperity spell, 108
protection against mis-
chievous spirits, 90
in rain ritual, 103
in seashore spell, 102
Small Folk chant, 86–87
to Water Faeries,
101–102
welcome to faery
garden, 165
children
brown dwarves and, 136
brownies and, 131
Fay, 58
Fay-human children,
51–52
first doorway and, 40
open to faeries, 11
in "Spring Equinox"
story, 178–180
China, 74–75, 139
chin-chin kobakama, 132
Chinese House Faery,
74–75, 118
Christianity, 3–4
cities, 12–13
closed door, 157
clouds, 156
clover, 161
Coblynaus, 132

colors, 41
companions, 62
Compassion, Law of, 80
cones, 167
cookies, 124–125
Cornwall (England)
Brown Men of, 143
knockers of, 144
pixies of, 148
shoney of, 143
council of elders
Fay councilors work
with, 62
of Schools of Learning,
58, 59
councilors, 62
cowslip, 161
crafts, 135, 136
craftspeople, 59–60
crystals, 93, 94
Cu Sith, 133
Cwn Anwnn, 38, 133

D
Daffodil (faery)
in "The Grain Mother"
story, 191–195
in "The Maiden's
Journey" story,
196–201
in "The Sacred Wedding"
story, 180–185
in "The Yule Faeries"
story, 201–205
daisy, 161
dance
blockages and, 84
with faeries, 31
to Fay, 69
by Small Folk, 76, 79
Dance of Life, 44
Dandelion (faery)
in "The Grain Mother"
story, 191–195

in "The Maiden's
Journey" story,
196–201
in "The Sacred
Wedding" story,
181–185
in "The Yule Faeries"
story, 201–205
dark elves, 57, 138
Dark Lord, 197, 198,
199, 200
days
doorways into Faery
Land on holy days,
37–38
special appearance times
of faeries, xii
times of day for finding
faeries, 10
times to see/communi-
cate with Small
Folk, 78
death
Cwn Anwnn and, 133
of faeries, 83
in "The Troll Tear" story,
201–205
in "The Yule Faeries"
story, 205–208
decoration, faery house,
168–170
Denmark, 140, 151
Desert Faeries, 113–115
desires, 99
Dionysus, 139
divination, 155–157
djinn (genies), 22–23,
114–115
dogs, 133
dollhouse, 169–170
domovoi, 25, 133–134
door, closed, 157
doorways, faery
Faery Rides and, 37–38
fifth doorway, 42–43
first doorway, 40

fourth doorway, 42
opening, 39–40
physical gate, 45–47
power spots, 45
second doorway, 40–41
seventh doorway, 44–45
sixth doorway, 43–44
third doorway, 41
dowsing rod, 45
dragons
description of, 134–135
of German faeries, 24
knowledge of magick, 5
as separate species from
faeries, 50
duendes, 25
duergar, 136
dwarves
of Bermuda, 25–26
description of, 135–137
knowledge of, 49
dwellings. *See also* house
of dwarves, 135
of Fay, 57–58
of gnomes, 140–141
of Small Folk, 78

E

Each Uisge, 137
earth, 140
Earth Faeries
faery ointment, 95–97
function of/powers of,
93–94
offering stone for good
luck, 94–95
Ebeltoft (Denmark), 136
Einstein, Albert, 11
elder, 163
Elder Blossom (faery)
in "The Grain Mother"
story, 191–195
in "The Maiden's
Journey" story,
196–201

in "The Sacred Wedding"
story, 180–185
in "The Yule Faeries"
story, 201–205
elementals
contacting faeries
through, 12
faeries *vs.*, 1–2
Fay and, 50
Elfhame, 53, 138
elves
description of, 137–139
Gianes, 140
knowledge/powers of, 49
light, dark elves, 53
living conditions of,
56, 57
in "The Sacred Wedding"
story, 180–185
emotions
anger, spell to dispel,
106–107
faeries and, 82–83
second faery doorway
and, 41
Water Faeries and, 101
energy lines, 45, 58
England
Brown Men of, 143
knockers of, 144
pixies of, 148
puca of, 149
shoney of, 143
Small Folk of, 76
enlightenment, 84
equinox
connection with faeries
during, 30–32
faery appearances at, xii
Faery Rides, 6, 37–38
"Spring Equinox" story,
177–180
"The Maiden's Journey"
story, 196–201
Ercildoune, Thomas
Rymour de, 54–55

European faeries, 23
European House Faery, 119

F

faeries. *See also* stories
Air Faeries, 99–100
calling to, 13
call within faery circle,
32–34
contacting through
meditation, 13–17
definition/description
of, 1–7
Desert Faeries, 113–115
D. J. Conway's life with,
xi–xiv
Earth Faeries, 93–97
finding, 10–13
Fire Faeries, 105–108
gardens, 159–165
greeting to, 31–32
holey stone use, 34–35
House Faeries, 117–125
Plant Faeries/Forest
Faeries, 109–111
in "The Sacred Wedding"
story, 180–185
seeing, rituals for, 17–19
vegetation and, 9
Water Faeries, 101–103
when they find you,
20–21
faeries, befriending
Air Faeries, 100
brownies, 22
Desert Faeries, 114
djinn, 22–23
Earth Faeries, 93
faeries around the world,
23–26
party for faeries, 26–27
pixies, 21
Small Folk, 76–77, 78
visiting faery home
meditation, 27–32
faery circle, 32–34

faery doorways. *See* doorways, faery
faery dust, 78
faery elixir potion, 18
Faery Folk, xi–xiv, 49–50
faery houses, 167–171
faery kith and kin
  barbegazi, 128–129
  boggarts, 130
  bogies, 129–130
  bokwus, 130
  brownies, 131–132
  chin-chin kobakama, 132
  Coblynaus, 132
  Cu Sith, 133
  Cwn Anwnn, 133
  domovoi, 133–134
  dragons, 134–135
  dwarves, 135–137
  Each Uisge, 137
  elves, 137–139
  fox spirits, 139
  in general, 127–128
  Gianes, 140
  gnomes, 140–141
  goblins, 141–142
  Green Man, 143
  gremlins, 142–143
  kelpies, 143–144
  knockers, 144
  kobolds, 145
  leshy or leshi, 145–146
  merfolk, 146
  ohdows, 147
  Pegasus, 147
  pixies, 148
  pookas, puca, Puck, 149
  Red Cap, 150
  ribhaus, 150
  selkies, 150–151
  trolls, 151–152
  uldra or *Huldra-Folk*, 152–153
  unicorns, 153
  urisk or *uruisg*, 154
  Wild Women, 154
Faery Land
  Elfhame, 53, 138
  existence of, 10–11
  faeries in, 1
  faery gardens, gateway to, 159, 160
  humans and, 6
  humans taken to, 54–56
  meeting faeries meditation, 14–17
  timelessness of, 80
  Tir-na-Nog ("Land of the Young"), 21
  visit to faery home, 27–32
  world of faeries, 3
Faery Land, opening door to
  calling magick from faery summer moon, 47–48
  faery doorways, 39–47
  Faery Rides, 37–38
faery magick, 6, 7. *See also* magickal uses
faery mounds, 56, 76
faery ointment, 95–97
faery oracle, 63, 155–157
Faery Rides
  connection with faeries during, 30–32
  description of, 6
  doorways to Faery Land, 37–38
  faery kith and kin on, 127–128
  humans on, 20–21
family, 117
Faroe Islands, 152
Fay
  avoidance of cities, 12–13
  bards, 61
  befriending, 9
  borrowing by, 87, 88
  calling guardian, 69–70
  call within faery circle, 32–34
  companions, 62
  councilors, 62
  dance/chant to, 69
  description of, 49–53
  D. J. Conway and, xi–xii
  faery doorways and, 42, 43, 44
  faery gifts, asking for, 70–72
  Faery Rides, 37–38
  as Fire Fairies, 105–106
  foretellers, 63
  greeting to faeries, 31
  guardians, 63
  guidance of Small Folk, 73
  healers, 63
  historians, 64
  hounds of, 133
  humans drawn into Faery Land by, 54–56
  interaction with, 7
  intermarriage with humans, 1
  living conditions of, 56–58
  magicians, 64
  meditation to, 66–68
  in meeting faeries meditation, 14, 17
  mystics, 64
  in protective circle, 85
  rituals taught by, 32
  Schools of Learning, 58–64
  Seelie and Unseelie Court, 53
  Small Folk *vs.*, 74
  teachers, 65
  types of, 3
  warriors, 65–66
  welcoming chant and, 87

fear, 4, 82
feathers, 156
fenoderee (Manx
  brownie), 131
fern, 162
fifth doorway, 42–43
Finland, 145
Fire Faeries, 105–108
Fire Glow, 187–189
first doorway, 40
flowers
  attraction of faeries
    with, 19
  faery, 161–163
  faery house welcoming
    ritual, 171
  Faery oracle, 156
Fluff (rabbit), 177–180
folletti, 24
food
  befriending faeries with,
    24, 25, 26
  cookies for brownies,
    124–125
  for faery garden welcome,
    164
  for faery party, 26
  offerings for faeries, 19
Forest Faeries, 109–111
forests
  elves and, 137
  Green Man and, 143
  leshi of, 145–146
foretellers, 63
fountain, 161
fourth doorway, 42
foxglove, 162
Fox Spirits, 139
France
  barbegazi of, 128–129
  faeries of, 24
  gommes of, 132
"friendly" faeries, 3, 4
friendship, 39–40. *See also*
  faeries, befriending

full moon
  asking for faery gifts
    on, 71
  calling magick from faery
    summer moon, 47–48
  House Faeries' celebra-
    tion at, 119
funeral, faery, 83
furnishings, faery house,
  168–170
future, 34

G
garden
  Plant Faeries and,
    109, 110
  Small Folk's relationship
    to, 81–82
gardens, faery
  elements of, 159–161
  flowers, 161–163
  stones, 164
  trees, 163–164
  welcome to, 164–165
gargoyles, 50, 118
gates. *See also* doorways,
  faery
  in faery garden, 159, 160
  into Faery Land, 10, 11,
    45–47
gazing balls, 159
genies (djinn), 22–23,
  114–115
Germany
  duergar mythology
    of, 136
  faeries of, 24
  gnomes of, 140, 141
  goblins of, 145
  Oak Men of, 143
  pookas of, 149
  Wichlein of, 132
  Wild Women of, 154
Gianes, 24, 140

gifts, faery, 70–72. *See also*
  offerings
ginger
  to attract faeries, 31
  for call within faery
    circle, 32
  for faery house welcom-
    ing ritual, 171
  for Small Folk chant, 86
gnomes, 24, 140–141
goblins, 141–142
God, 80
Goddess, 80, 180–185
gommes, 132
"The Grain Mother",
  191–195
Green Leaf, 173–176
Green Man, 143
gremlins, 142–143
guardians
  calling Fay guardian,
    69–70
  faeries as, 10
  Fay as, 63
  Small Folk as, 74
guides, 10, 74

H
Halloween, 201–205.
  See also Samhain
  (October 31)
harvest, 191–195
Hawaii, 23–24
hawthorn, 163–164
hazel, 164
Healer-Monitors, 60, 65
healers, 63
heather, 162
historians, 64
holey stone, 34–35
Hollow Men, 152
hollyhock, 162
holy days. *See also* stories
  appearance of faeries
    on, xii

(holy days, *continued*)
 connection with faeries
  on, 30–32
 doorways into Faery
  Land on, 37–38
 Faery Rides on, 6,
  127–128
home. *See* house
horses
 djinn and, 23
 faeries' love of, 5–6
 faery horses, 20–21
 lutins in form of, 24
 Pegasus, 147
 phouka, 149
hounds, 133
hours of the day, xii, 78
house
 attracting faeries into, 19
 chin-chin kobakama
  and, 132
 expelling harmful
  faeries, 85
 faery houses, 167–171
 of Fay, 57–58
 House Faeries, 117–125
 protection against mis-
  chievous spirits,
  89–90
 repelling negative faeries,
  19–20
 Small Folk and, 75
House Faeries
 description of, 117–119
 invitation ritual,
  120–121
 meditation, 121–123
 spell for brownies,
  124–125
 welcoming ritual,
  123–124
Huldra-Folk, 152–153
humans
 Air Faeries and, 99
 brownies and, 131

Earth Faeries and, 93
faery guides/guardians
 for, 10
faery kith and kin,
 respect for, 127
in Faery Land, 6, 54–56
Fay alliances with, 51–52
Fay appearance similar
 to, 49
Fay bards and, 61
Fay companions and, 62
Fay laws and, 52
Fay teachers and, 65
Fay warriors and, 65–66
Forest Faeries and, 110
gnomes and, 141
Green Man and, 143
gremlins and, 142
House Faeries and,
 117–125
intermarriage with Fay, 1
kelpies and, 143–144
knockers and, 144
kobolds and, 145
merfolk and, 146
pixies and, 148
Plant Faeries and, 109
pookas, pucas, Puck and,
 149, 150
Red Cap and, 150
relationship with faeries,
 2–7
selkies and, 150–151
Small Folk and, 74–75
in "Spring Equinox"
 story, 178–180
trolls and, 151–152
Water Faeries and, 101

I
Iceland
 dwarves of, 136
 illes of, 151–152
 puki of, 149
illes, 151–152

Imbolc (February 1)
 appearance of faeries
  on, xii
 greeting to faeries, 31
 "The Wizard and the
  Spring Maiden" story,
  173–176
Inari (Fox Spirit), 139
India
 faeries of, 25
 Kubera of, 135–136
 ribhaus of, 150
indoor potted plants, 9
inner seeing, 42
intellect, 105
intuition, 55–56
invitation
 to faery garden, 164–165
 House Faery ritual,
  120–121
Ireland
 ballybogs of, 129
 Faery Rides, 20–21
 merrow of, 146
 phouka of, 149
 Small Folk of, 76–77
iron
 faery rituals and, 17
 Fay blacksmithing
  and, 60
 poisonous to Faery Folk,
  5–6
Islam, 3–4
Italy, 24, 140

J
Janet, 55
Japan
 chin-chin kobakama
  of, 132
 Fox Spirits of, 139
 Small Folk of, 75
Japanese Snow Queen, 75
jasmine, 84, 162

"Jason and the Faery Ring",
    185–191
jewelry
    for calling magick from
        faery summer moon
        ritual, 47, 48
    by djinn, 23
    by dwarves, 135, 137
journal
    after visit to faery home,
        27–32
    for recording meditation
        experiences, 13, 17
    singing in, 84
Judaism, 3–4
June, 76

K

kelpies, 143–144
key, 157
kidnapping, 55–56, 76
kin. See faery kith and kin
kings
    of elves, 138
    Faery Rides and, 38
    of Fay and elves, 56, 57
    of Small Folk, 15–16
Kirk, Robert, 55–56
kith. See faery kith and kin
knackers, 144
knockers, 144
kobito (Japanese faery), 75
kobolds, 145
Korea, 76
Kuang-han kung (Palace
    of the Boundless
    Cold), 75
Kubera (Hindu god),
    135–136

L

Lammas (August 1),
    191–195
land development, 82

Land of the Niebelungen,
    135
"Land of the Young"
    (Tir-na-Nog), 21
Lapland, 152
Latin America, 25–26
Law of Beauty, 80–81
Law of Compassion, 80
Law of Power, 80
laws
    of Fay, 52
    of Small Folk, 74,
        79–81, 83
leaf, 156
learning. See Schools of
    Learning
leprechaun, 77, 117
leshi, 145–146
leshy, 25, 145–146
ley lines, 58
lie, 119
life span
    of elves, 138
    of faeries, 83
    of Fox Spirits, 139
light elves, 138
lilac, 162
Lilac (faery)
    in "The Grain Mother"
        story, 191–195
    in "The Maiden's
        Journey" story,
        196–201
    in "The Sacred Wedding"
        story, 181–185
    in "The Yule Faeries"
        story, 201–205
listening, 41
living conditions, 56–58
Lord of the Greenwood,
    180–185
love
    praise and, 82–83
    request for new love, 91
    seventh doorway and, 44

luck, 94–95
Lunasa (August 1)
    appearance of faeries
        on, xii
    "The Grain Mother"
        story, 191–195
    greeting to faeries, 31
lutins, 24

M

magicians, 64
magick
    D. J. Conway's life with,
        xi–xiv
    faery magick, 6, 7
    power of, 82
magickal uses
    of barbegazi, 129
    of boggarts, 130
    of bogies, 130
    of bokwus, 130
    of brownies, 132
    of chin-chin kobakama,
        132
    of Coblynaus, 132
    of Cu Sith, 133
    of Cwn Anwnn, 133
    of domovoi, 134
    of dragons, 134–135
    of dwarves, 137
    of Each Uisge, 137
    of elves, 138
    of Fox Spirits, 139
    of Gianes, 140
    of gnomes, 141
    of goblins, 142
    of Green Man, 143
    of gremlins, 143
    of kelpies, 144
    of knockers, 144
    of kobolds, 145
    of leshi or leshy, 146
    of merfolk, 146
    of ohdows, 147
    of Pegasus, 147

(magickal uses, *continued*)
  of pixies, 148
  of Puck, 149
  of Red Cap, 150
  of *ribhaus*, 150
  of selkies, 151
  of trolls, 152
  of *uldra* or Huldra-
    Folk, 153
  of unicorns, 153
  of *urisk*, 154
  use of term, 128
  of Wild Women, 154
"The Maiden's Journey",
  196–201
making love, 83
marigold, 162
masters, 58–59
May, 76
Meadow-Grass (faery)
  in "The Grain Mother"
    story, 191–195
  in "The Maiden's
    Journey" story,
    196–201
  in "The Sacred Wedding"
    story, 180–185
  in "The Yule Faeries"
    story, 201–205
meditation
  for contacting faeries, 84
  of faery doorways, 39
  Faery oracle, 155
  to Fay, 66–68
  House Faery meditation,
    121–123
  meeting faeries through,
    13–17
  negative faeries during,
    20
  release of anger, 107
  visit to faery home,
    27–32
menehune, 23–24
merfolk, 146

merrow, 146
metallurgy, 135, 136, 137
Mexico, 26
mice, 118
mind, 39
mining, 144, 145
mirror
  in faery garden, 159
  for faery party, 26
  in home for faeries, 12
mischievous spirits. *See also*
    trickster faeries
  bogies, 129–130
  gnomes, 141–142
  pixies, 148
  protection against, 89–90
moon
  calling magick from faery
    summer moon, 47–48
  faery gifts request on full
    moon, 71
  Faery oracle, 156
  House Faeries' celebra-
    tion, 119
Moor Men, 143
Mother
  "The Grain Mother",
    191–195
  in "The Troll Tear" story,
    202
  in "The Yule Faeries"
    story, 207–208
mountain, 156
mugwort, 162
music, 61
mystics, 44, 64

N
names, 2–3
Native American culture
  bokwus and, 130
  faeries and, 82
  ohdows of, 147
natural disasters, 93–94,
  147

nature
  befriending faeries and,
    9–10
  elves and, 137
  faeries as custodians of, 4
  faery sightings in, 84
  Fay guardians and, 63
  Green Man and, 143
  learning from Small Folk
    about, 85
  Plant/Forest Faeries,
    109–111
  second faery doorway
    and, 40–41
  Small Folk laws and,
    80–81
  working with Small Folk
    and, 77–78
negative faeries. *See*
  "unfriendly" faeries
Netherlands, 24
New Zealand, 23, 136
Norway, 140, 152–153

O
oak, 164
Oak Men, 143
offerings
  befriending faeries with,
    24, 25, 26
  to faeries, 19
  to House Faeries, 120
  to Small Folk, 76–77
offering stone, 94–95
ohdows, 147
ointment, faery, 95–97
Old Path (Wicca), xiii
Old Wise One, 197,
  198–200
oracle, faery, 63, 155–157
Oriental dragon, 134
Otherworld, 2, 10–11. *See
  also* Faery Land

P

Pacific Islands, 23
Palace of the Boundless
Cold (*Kuang-han
kung*), 75
pansy, 162
para, 145
Paracelsus, 138
party, 26–27, 76
passion, 83
past, 34
path, faery garden,
159, 160
Pegasus, 147
pendulum, 45
peony, 162
personality traits
of *barbegazi*, 129
of *boggarts*, 130
of bogies, 130
of *bokwus*, 130
of brownies, 132
of chin-chin kobakama,
132
of *Coblynaus*, 132
of *Cu Sith*, 133
of *Cwn Anwnn*, 133
of *domovoi*, 134
of dragons, 135
of dwarves, 137
of *Each Uisge*, 137
of elves, 139
of entities, 127
of Fox Spirits, 139
of *Gianes*, 140
of gnomes, 141
of goblins, 142
of Green Man, 143
of gremlins, 143
of kelpies, 144
of knockers, 144
of kobolds, 145
of *leshi* or *leshy*, 146
of merfolk, 146

of *ohdows*, 147
of Pegasus, 147
of pixies, 148
of Puck, 149
of Red Cap, 150
of *ribhaus*, 150
of selkies, 151
of trolls, 152
of *uldra* or Huldra-
Folk, 153
of unicorns, 153
of *urisk*, 154
use of term, 128
of Wild Women, 154
phouka, 149
pixies, 21, 148
Plant Faeries, 109–111
plants
attraction of faeries
with, 19
Desert Faeries and,
113–114
elves and, 137
faeries and, 9
faery gardens, 159–165
House Faeries and, 118
second faery doorway
and, 40–41
Small Folk's relationship
to, 81–82
pleasure, 81–82
ponaturi (Sea Faeries), 23
pookas, 149
poppy, 162
potion, faery elixir, 18
potted plants, 159–160
potting soil, 159
Power, Law of, 80
power spots, 45–47
praise
of brownies, 124
love and, 82–83
by Small Folk, 77, 78
primrose, 162–163
prosperity spell, 107–108

puca, 149
Puck, 149
puki, 149
pussywillow, 163

Q

queen
of elves, 138
Faery Rides and, 38
of Fay, 54, 55, 57
of Fay and elves, 56
of Small Folk, 15–16
Queen of the May,
180–185

R

Rades. *See* Faery Rides
rain ritual, 103
recipe, faery ointment,
95–97
Red Cap, 150
religion, 3–4
Rhythm, Universal, 79
ribhaus, 150
Rides. *See* Faery Rides
rituals
calling Fay guardian,
69–70
calling magick from faery
summer moon, 47–48
call within faery circle,
32–34
contacting faeries
through, 84
dance/chant to Fay, 69
djinn, wishes granted by,
114–115
faery gifts, asking for,
70–72
faery house welcoming
ritual, 171
greeting to faeries, 31–32
House Faeries, welcom-
ing, 123–124

(rituals, *continued*)
House Faery ritual,
120–121
meditation to Fay, 66–68
mischievous spirits, pro-
tection against, 89–90
new love, request for, 91
offering stone for good
luck, 94–95
for rain, 103
seashore spell, 102–103
for seeing faeries, 17–19
Small Folk chant, 86–87
spell to recover borrowed
objects, 87–89
river, 156
Rose (faery)
in "The Grain Mother"
story, 191–195
in "The Maiden's
Journey" story,
196–201
in "The Sacred Wedding"
story, 180–185
in "The Yule Faeries"
story, 201–205
rosemary, 163
rowan, 164
Rugen, 136–137
Russia, 25, 133–134
Rymour de Ercildoune,
Thomas, 54–55

S

"The Sacred Wedding",
180–185
Samhain (October 31)
appearance of faeries
on, xii
greeting to faeries, 31
"The Troll Tear" story,
201–205
Scandinavia
dwarves of, 135
Elfhame word from, 53

elves from, 137
faery islands, 24
Oak Men of, 143
pookas of, 149
trolls from, 151
Schools of Learning
classes of study in, 61
companions, 62
councilors, 62
description of, 57, 58–60
Fay bards, 61
foretellers, 63
guardians, 63
healers, 63
historians, 64
magicians, 64
mystics, 64
teachers, 65
warriors, 65–66
Scotland
boggarts of, 130
brownies of, 131
Brown Men of, 143
Cu Sith of, 133
Each Uisge of, 137
gnomes of, 141
kelpies of, 143
urisk of, 154
seashore spell, 102–103
second doorway, 40–41
Second Sight, 55–56
*The Secret Commonwealth
of Elves, Fauns and
Fairies* (Kirk), 55–56
secret faery oracle, 63,
155–157
seeing
faery sightings, 84
fourth doorway is, 42
House Faeries, 119
seer's method to see
faeries, 87
Seelie Court (Blessed
Court)
description of, 3
explanation of, 56–60

Fay characteristics, 53
Fay from, 51
Fay laws, 52
Fay roles, 61–66
selkies, 150–151
seventh doorway, 44–45
shape-shifting, 93
shoney, 143–144
Sicily, 24
silence, 43
singing
of House Faeries, 119
in journal, 84
making love as, 83
sink stone, 47, 48
sixth doorway, 43–44
Small Folk
borrowed objects, spell to
recover, 87–89
call within faery circle,
32–34
contacting, 84–85
description of, 73–74
D. J. Conway's life
with, xii
faery doorways and,
40–45
Faery Rides, 37–38
Fay and, 49–50
Fay teachers for, 65
finding, 10–12
greeting to faeries, 31–32
Healer-Monitors and, 60
holey stone use, 34–35
as House Faeries, 117
laws of, 52, 79–81
life/experiences of, 82–84
love of horses, 5–6
in meeting faeries
meditation, 14–17
new love, request for, 91
pixies and, 148
plants and, 9
pleasure and, 81–82
prosperity spell, 107–108

protection against mis-
chievous spirits,
89–90
types of faeries, world-
wide, 74–77
use of term, 3
visiting faery home medi-
tation, 27–32
welcoming chant, 86–87
working with, 77–79
Socrates, 138
solitary faeries, 85,
110–111
solstice
connection with faeries
during, 30–32
Faery Rides, 6, 37–38
"Jason and the Faery
Ring" story, 185–191
"The Yule Faeries" story,
205–208
sound, 41
spells
anger, dispelling,
106–107
borrowed objects, recov-
ering, 87–89
for brownies, 124–125
Faery oracle, 155–157
prosperity spell, 107–108
seashore spell, 102–103
spiritual development,
101, 153
"Spring Equinox",
177–180
Spring equinox (March)
faery appearances at, xii
greeting to faeries, 31
"Spring Equinox" story,
177–180
Spring Maiden
"Spring Equinox" story,
177–180
"The Wizard and the
Spring Maiden" story,
173–176

stars, 156
statues, 161
stillness, 43
stone
faery gift, 70–71
Faery oracle, 155–156
faery ritual with, 17–18
faery stones, 164
holey stone, 34–35
offering stone for good
luck, 94–95
sink stone, 47, 48
stories
"The Grain Mother",
191–195
"Jason and the Faery
Ring", 185–191
"The Maiden's Journey",
196–201
"The Sacred Wedding",
180–185
"Spring Equinox",
177–180
"The Troll Tear",
201–205
"The Wizard and the
Spring Maiden",
173–176
"The Yule Faeries",
205–208
storms, 99
strawberry, 163
Summerland, 53
summer solstice
calling magick from faery
summer moon, 47–48
greeting to faeries, 31
"Jason and the Faery
Ring" story, 185–191
sun, 156
Sun King
in "Spring Equinox"
story, 178–180
in "The Wizard and the
Spring Maiden" story,
174, 175–176

in "The Yule Faeries"
story, 205–208
surrender, 80–81
Sweden, 140, 151
Switzerland, 128–129
sword, 156

T

Tam Lin, 55
teachers, 65, 71–72
tengu (Japanese faery), 75
terrarium, 160
"Thomas the Rhymer"
(poem), 54–55
thyme, 163
time
Faery Land and, 6
for finding faeries, 10, 78
Law of Power and, 80
Tir-na-Nog ("Land of the
Young"), 21
treasure chest, open, 157
tree, 156
trees, faery, 163–164
trellis, 159, 160
trickster faeries. *See also*
mischievous spirits
conversation with, 19
dealing with, 20
Fox Spirits, 139
trolls, 151–152
"The Troll Tear", 201–205

U

uldra, 152–153
Unblessed Court. *See*
Unseelie Court
"unfriendly" faeries
expelling from home, 85
humans and, 3
leshy, 25
mischievous spirits, pro-
tection against, 89–90
repelling, 19–20
types of, 4

"unfriendly" faery kith
and kin
dwarves, 136–137
goblins, 141–142
gremlins, 142–143
kelpies, 143–144
kobolds, 145
leshi or *leshy*, 145–146
Red Cap, 150
unicorns, 153
universal energy, 93–94,
140–141
Universal Rhythm, 79
Unseelie Court (Unblessed
Court)
bards, 61
description of, 3
Fay characteristics, 53
Fay from, 51
Fay, help from, 66
Fay laws, 52
Fay living conditions,
56–57
Schools of Learning
and, 58
urisk, 154
uruisg, 154

V
vermiculite, 159
vervain, 163
vibrations
faery doorways and,
40, 42
House Faeries and, 123
vines, 160, 168

W
Wales
brownie of, 131
Coblynaus of, 132
Cwn Anwnn of, 133
pookas of, 149
wand, 156
warriors, 60, 65–66
wars, 60
water
in calling magick from
faery summer moon
ritual, 47–48
Fox Spirit and, 139
for House Faeries, 124
leshy and, 146
merfolk and, 146
offerings for faeries, 19
selkies and, 150–151
Water Faeries
chant to, 102
function of, 101
ritual for rain, 103
seashore spell, 102–103
water-horse, 137
Water of Life, 101, 102
weather
Air Faeries and, 99
faeries that control,
23, 24
rain ritual, 103
Water Faeries' control
of, 101
wedding, "The Sacred
Wedding", 180–185
welcoming ritual
for faery garden,
164–165

for faery house, 171
for House Faeries,
123–124
Western dragon, 134
white dwarves, 136
white feather, 156
Wicca (Old Path), xiii
Wichlein, 132
Wild Women, 154
willow, 164
wind, 99
winged bulls, 50
wings
of Desert Faeries, 113
of dragons, 134
Fay do not have, 53
of Pegasus, 147
of Small Folk, 10, 73–74
of *tengu*, 75
winter solstice
appearance of faeries
on, xii
greeting to faeries, 31
"The Yule Faeries" story,
205–208
Wise Old One, 207
wishes, 114–115
"The Wizard and the
Spring Maiden",
173–176
work, 4
wronged-love, 82
Wunderburg, 154

Y
"The Yule Faeries",
205–208

Printed in the United States
by Baker & Taylor Publisher Services